WeightWatchers®

Satisfying, speedy recipes for everyday

Meals in 30 Minutes

D0183445

First published in Great Britain by Simon & Schuster UK Ltd, 2014
A CBS Company

Copyright © 2014, Weight Watchers International, Inc.
Simon & Schuster Illustrated Books, Simon & Schuster UK Ltd,
First Floor, 222 Gray's Inn Road, London WC1X 8HB

www.simonandschuster.co.uk

Simon & Schuster Australia, Sydney
Simon & Schuster India, New Delhi

Weight Watchers, **ProPoints** and the **ProPoints** icon are the registered trademarks
of Weight Watchers International Inc. and are used under license by Weight Watchers
(UK) Ltd.

Weight Watchers Publications: Lucy Clements, Imogen Prescott, Nina McKerlie.

Recipes written by: Sue Ashworth, Sue Beveridge, Sara Buenfeld,
Tamsin Burnett-Hall, Cas Clarke, Siân Davies, Roz Denny, Nicola Graimes,
Becky Johnson, Kim Morphew, Joy Skipper, Penny Stephens and Wendy Veale
as well as Weight Watchers Leaders and Members.

Photography by: Iain Bagwell, Steve Baxter, Will Heap, Steve Lee, Lis Parsons,
Juliet Piddington and William Shaw.
Project editor: Sharon Amos.
Design and typesetting: Geoff Fennell.
Proofreading: Jane Bamforth.

Printed and bound in China.

A CIP catalogue record for this book is available from the British Library

ISBN 978-1-47113-167-7

10 9 8 7 6 5 4 3 2 1

Pictured on the title page: Jambalaya p40.
Pictured on the Introduction: Root vegetable rösti with poached egg p144, Rosemary
lamb fillets p78, Apple and raspberry muffins p156.

WeightWatchers®

Satisfying, speedy recipes for everyday

Meals in 30 Minutes

SIMON &
SCHUSTER
ILLUSTRATED

London · New York · Sydney · Toronto · New Delhi

A CBS COMPANY

If you would like to find out more about Weight Watchers and the **ProPoints** Plan, please visit: www.weightwatchers.co.uk

Ⓥ This symbol denotes a vegetarian recipe and assumes that, where relevant, free range eggs, vegetarian cheese, vegetarian virtually fat free fromage frais, vegetarian low fat crème fraîche and vegetarian low fat yogurts are used. Virtually fat free fromage frais, low fat crème fraîche and low fat yogurts may contain traces of gelatine so they are not always vegetarian. Please check the labels.

❄ This symbol denotes a dish that can be frozen. Unless otherwise stated, you can freeze the finished dish for up to 3 months. Defrost thoroughly and reheat until the dish is piping hot throughout.

Recipe notes

Egg size: Medium, unless otherwise stated.

Raw eggs: Only the freshest eggs should be used. Pregnant women, the elderly and children should avoid recipes with eggs that are not fully cooked or raw.

All fruits and vegetables: Medium, unless otherwise stated.

Stock: Stock cubes are used in recipes, unless otherwise stated. These should be prepared according to packet instructions.

Timings: These are approximate and meant to be guidelines.

Microwaves: Timings and temperatures are for a standard 800 W microwave. If necessary, adjust your own microwave.

Low fat spread: Where a recipe states to use a low fat spread, a light spread with a fat content of no less than 38% should be used.

Low fat soft cheese: Where low fat soft cheese is specified in a recipe, this refers to soft cheese with a fat content of less than 5%.

ProPoints values: Should you require the **ProPoints** values for any of the recipes within this book, you can call Customer Services on 0845 345 1500 and we will provide you with the relevant information on a recipe-by-recipe basis. Please allow 28 days for us to provide you with this information.

Contents

Introduction

We're all so busy these days that to have to cook dinner from scratch after a hectic day can feel like the final straw. It's so tempting to reach for a ready-meal or order a take-away. But these recipes will prove to you that it is possible to put a filling, nutritious home cooked meal on the table in just 30 minutes – a welcome thought after a long day.

You'll find warming meal-in-a-bowl soups such as Chicken and Corn Chowder or Prawn and Crab Soup, and delicious salads like Fresh Tuna Niçoise or Bacon and Spinach. Instead of a take-away, just turn to dishes such as Chicken Chow Mein and Chicken Korma and see how easy it is to cook your own. If you're entertaining mid-week, why not try Beef Tataki or Japanese-style Fondue? And for sheer comfort food you can't beat family favourites like Speedy Shepherd's Pie, Bangers and Mash with Onion Gravy or Macaroni Cheese – all on the table in half an hour. Vegetarians will enjoy an amazingly quick Butternut Squash, Spinach and Feta Lasagne among other delights, and we haven't forgotten desserts and treats – you'll find quick and easy recipes for muffins, plus Raspberry Tarts, Cherry Scones and a classic Baked Alaska.

About Weight Watchers

For more than 40 years Weight Watchers has been helping people around the world to lose weight using a long term sustainable approach. Weight Watchers successful weight loss system is based on four tried and trusted principles:

- Eating healthily
- Being more active
- Adjusting behaviour to help weight loss
- Getting support in weekly meetings

Our unique **ProPoints** system empowers you to manage your food plan and make wise recipe choices for a healthier, happier you.

Storing and freezing

Many dishes store well in the fridge, but make sure you use them up within a day or two. Some can also be frozen. However, it is important to make sure you know how to freeze and defrost different types of food safely.

- Wrap any food to be frozen in rigid containers or strong freezer bags. This is important to stop foods contaminating each other or getting freezer burn.
- Label the containers or bags with the contents and date – your freezer should have a star marking that tells you how long you can keep different types of frozen food.
- Never freeze warm food – always let it cool completely first.
- Never freeze food that has already been frozen and defrosted.
- Freeze food in portions, then you can take out as little or as much as you need each time.
- Fresh food, such as raw chicken or fish, should be wrapped and frozen as soon as possible after buying.
- Most fruit and vegetables can be frozen by open freezing. Lay them out on a tray, freeze until solid and then pack them into bags.
- Some vegetables, such as peas, broccoli and broad beans can be blanched first by cooking for 2 minutes in boiling water. Drain, refresh under cold water and then freeze once cold.
- Fresh herbs are great frozen – either seal leaves in bags or, for soft herbs such as basil and parsley, chop finely and add to ice cube trays with water. These are

great for dropping into casseroles or soups straight from the freezer.

● Defrost what you need in the fridge, making sure you put anything that might have juices, such as meat, on a covered plate or in a container.

Some things cannot be frozen. Whole eggs do not freeze well, but yolks and whites can be frozen separately. Vegetables with a high water content, such as salad leaves, celery and cucumber, will not freeze. Fried foods will be soggy if frozen, and sauces such as mayonnaise will separate when thawed and should not be frozen.

Shopping hints and tips

Always buy the best ingredients you can afford. If you are going to cook healthy meals, it is worth investing in some quality ingredients that will really add flavour to your dishes. When buying meat, choose lean cuts of meat or lean mince, and if you are buying prepacked cooked sliced meat, buy it fresh from the deli counter.

When you're going around the supermarket it's tempting to pick up foods you like and put them in your trolley without thinking about how you will use them. So, a good plan is to decide what dishes you want to cook before you go shopping, check your store cupboard and make a list of what you need. You'll save time (and money) by not drifting aimlessly around the supermarket picking up what you fancy.

We've added a checklist here for some common storecupboard ingredients. Just add fresh ingredients to your regular shop and you'll be ready to cook.

Storecupboard checklist

- [ ] almonds, ground
- [ ] apricots, dried, ready-to-eat
- [ ] artificial sweetener, granulated
- [ ] baking powder
- [ ] bay leaves
- [ ] bicarbonate of soda
- [ ] black eyed beans, canned
- [ ] bran flakes
- [ ] bulgur wheat
- [ ] butter beans, canned
- [ ] Cajun spice mix
- [ ] capers
- [ ] caraway seeds
- [ ] cardamom pods
- [ ] chick peas, canned
- [ ] chilli flakes
- [ ] chilli powder
- [ ] chilli sauce
- [ ] Chinese five spice
- [ ] Chinese plum sauce
- [ ] cinnamon, ground and sticks
- [ ] cocoa
- [ ] coconut milk, reduced fat
- [ ] cooking spray, calorie controlled
- [ ] coriander, ground and seeds
- [ ] cornflour
- [ ] couscous, dried

- [ ] cream of tartar
- [ ] crispbreads (wholewheat)
- [ ] cumin, ground and seeds
- [ ] curry (paste and powder)
- [ ] dried exotic fruits, ready-to-eat
- [ ] fajita seasoning
- [ ] fish sauce
- [ ] flour, plain, self-raising and wholemeal
- [ ] gherkins
- [ ] glacé cherries
- [ ] grape nuts
- [ ] harissa paste
- [ ] hazelnut chocolate spread
- [ ] herbs, dried
- [ ] honey, clear
- [ ] horseradish sauce
- [ ] jerk seasoning
- [ ] kidney beans, canned
- [ ] mayonnaise, extra light
- [ ] mustard
- [ ] noodles
- [ ] nutmeg
- [ ] oil (vegetable, olive, walnut, sesame)
- [ ] olives in brine, black
- [ ] oyster sauce
- [ ] paprika
- [ ] pasta, dried

- [ ] peanuts, roasted
- [ ] peppercorns
- [ ] peppers, flame-roasted, in a jar
- [ ] pesto, reduced fat
- [ ] piccalilli
- [ ] pineapple, canned in natural juice
- [ ] porridge oats
- [ ] Puy lentils
- [ ] raisins
- [ ] ras el hanout
- [ ] raspberry jam
- [ ] rice, dried
- [ ] rolled oats
- [ ] sesame seeds
- [ ] sherry
- [ ] soy sauce
- [ ] stock cubes
- [ ] sun-dried tomato paste
- [ ] sweetcorn, canned
- [ ] tomato ketchup
- [ ] tomato purée
- [ ] tomatoes, canned
- [ ] turmeric
- [ ] vanilla extract
- [ ] vinegar (balsamic, wine, rice)
- [ ] Worcestershire sauce

Soups and salads

Courgette, pea and mint soup

Serves 4

159 calories per serving

Ⓥ

❄

calorie controlled cooking
   spray
2 leeks, chopped roughly
2 courgettes, cubed
700 ml (1¼ pints) hot
   vegetable stock
400 g (14 oz) potatoes, cubed
300 ml (10 fl oz) skimmed milk
150 g (5½ oz) frozen peas
3 heaped tablespoons
   chopped fresh mint
juice of ½ a lemon
freshly ground black pepper

This velvety, green soup has a fresh and summery flavour.

1 Spray a large, lidded saucepan with the cooking spray. Add the leeks and cook, stirring, for 3 minutes. Add the courgettes and 4 tablespoons of the stock. Cover and cook for 3 minutes. Mix in the potatoes and the rest of the stock, plus the milk. Bring to the boil and simmer, partially covered, for 12 minutes or until the potatoes are tender.

2 Add the peas and mint to the pan and cook for 2 minutes more. Transfer the soup to a liquidiser, or use a hand held blender, and blend until smooth, adding the lemon juice and black pepper to taste. Return to the pan and reheat if necessary and serve in warm bowls.

Chicken and corn chowder

Serves 2
260 calories per serving
❄ (without the potatoes)

calorie controlled cooking spray
150 g (5½ oz) skinless chicken breast fillet, cubed
1 medium leek, trimmed, cleaned and chopped
250 g (9 oz) potatoes, cubed
425 ml (15 fl oz) chicken stock
100 g (3½ oz) baby corn, sliced
300 ml (10 fl oz) skimmed milk
salt and freshly ground black pepper

A chunky soup that will fill you up fast.

1 Heat a lidded, non-stick frying pan, spray with the cooking spray and brown the chicken over a medium heat for 2 minutes or until beginning to colour.

2 Add the leek and seasoning, cover the pan, and cook for 2 minutes. Stir in the potatoes and stock, then simmer, covered, for 10 minutes.

3 Mix in the corn and milk, return to the boil, and simmer for 5 minutes partially covered. Ladle into warm bowls to serve.

Prawn and crab soup

Serves 2
469 calories per serving

Deliciously light yet rich, this main meal soup makes a great simple lunch or supper dish. Don't be put off by the length of the ingredients list – it really is a very easy recipe to make.

75 g (2¾ oz) dried vermicelli noodles

calorie controlled cooking spray

2 garlic cloves, chopped

1 teaspoon chopped fresh root ginger

a stalk of lemongrass, chopped finely

500 ml (18 fl oz) fish stock

1 tablespoon Thai fish sauce

juice of ½ a lime

3 tablespoons reduced fat coconut milk

4 baby corn, sliced diagonally

2 spring onions, sliced diagonally

2 tablespoons chopped fresh coriander

½ red chilli, de-seeded and chopped finely

50 g (1¾ oz) baby spinach leaves, stems trimmed

125 g (4½ oz) canned white crab meat in brine, drained

150 g (5½ oz) frozen cooked prawns

salt and freshly ground black pepper

1 Bring a pan of water to the boil, add the noodles and cook according to the packet instructions then drain and refresh under cold running water. Drain again and set aside.

2 Heat a large non-stick saucepan, spray with the cooking spray and add the garlic, ginger and lemongrass. Fry for a minute before adding the stock and fish sauce. Bring to the boil then reduce the heat and simmer for 5 minutes.

3 Add the lime juice, coconut milk, baby corn, spring onions, half of the coriander, chilli, spinach and crab meat. Simmer over a medium-low heat for 2 minutes, then add the prawns and cook for another 4–5 minutes.

4 Divide the noodles between two large, shallow bowls and ladle over the soup. Season and serve sprinkled with the remaining coriander.

Carrot and ginger soup

Serves 6
53 calories per serving

calorie controlled cooking
  spray
2 onions, chopped
3 garlic cloves, chopped
500 g (1 lb 2 oz) carrots,
  peeled and chopped
6 cm (2½ inches) fresh root
  ginger, peeled and chopped
2 bay leaves
2.5 litres (4½ pints) hot
  vegetable stock

*This soup is just the right colour to serve at Halloween and
the ginger adds a great zing.*

1 Spray a large lidded saucepan with the cooking spray and
heat until hot. Add the onions and stir-fry for 5 minutes, then
stir in the garlic, carrots, ginger and bay leaves and cook for
1 more minute before adding the stock. Bring to the boil, cover
and simmer for 20 minutes until tender.

2 Remove from the heat, take out the bay leaves and transfer
to a food processor or use a hand held blender in the pan.
Blend until smooth (you may have to do this in batches). Return
to the pan to heat through. Serve in warm bowls or in mugs.

Variation... Use the same amount of parsnips instead of
the carrots.

French onion soup

Serves 2

57 calories per serving

Ⓥ

calorie controlled cooking
 spray

2 onions, sliced finely (about
 250 g/9 oz)

1 tablespoon fresh thyme
 leaves

450 ml (16 fl oz) vegetable
 stock

1 large tomato, de-seeded and
 cubed

salt and freshly ground black
 pepper

*The secret to perfect onion soup is to let the onions cook
very slowly, until they have released their natural sugars
and become caramelised.*

1 Heat a wide, deep, lidded, non-stick saucepan and spray
with the cooking spray. Add the onions and thyme and cook
very slowly, covered, for 20 minutes, stirring occasionally, until
the onions have caramelised and softened. If the onions begin
to stick, just add a few splashes of water to loosen them.

2 Pour in the vegetable stock and bring to the boil. Season
generously then ladle into shallow bowls and top with the
cubed tomato. Serve immediately.

Tip... You could try serving this soup with a 20 g (¾ oz)
slice of French stick per person, sprinkled with 10 g (¼ oz)
grated Gruyère cheese and grilled lightly until melted.

Chicken with orange and fennel salad

Serves 2
178 calories per serving

2 x 165 g (5¾ oz) skinless, boneless chicken breasts
calorie controlled cooking spray
1 teaspoon finely chopped fresh rosemary or fresh thyme
salt and freshly ground black pepper

For the salad
1 large orange
1 small red onion, sliced thinly
1 small fennel bulb, sliced thinly
½ teaspoon cumin seeds, toasted (see Tip)
2 teaspoons red or white wine vinegar

A refreshing salad served with herb-scented chicken.

1 Preheat the grill to a medium-high heat. Place the chicken between two pieces of cling film and bash to an even thickness. Spray the chicken with the cooking spray, season, then rub in the chopped rosemary or thyme.

2 Grill the chicken breasts for 12–15 minutes, turning occasionally, until thoroughly cooked. (Check by inserting a sharp knife into the chicken – the juices should run clear if it is cooked. If not, cook for a little longer.)

3 Meanwhile, prepare the salad. Using a sharp knife, remove all the peel and pith from the orange. Do this over a bowl to catch the juice, which is needed for the dressing. Cut the orange into segments, removing all the pith, and add to the bowl.

4 Add the onion, fennel, cumin seeds and vinegar to the oranges, tossing everything together gently to combine. Season, then pile on to two plates and serve with the hot chicken breasts, spooning some of the dressing over them.

Tips... To toast the cumin seeds, put them in a dry non-stick frying pan and cook them over a medium heat for 1–2 minutes, stirring often.

If you prefer, substitute some sliced celery or carrot for the red onion.

Greek summer vegetable salad

Serves 4
165 calories per serving
Ⓨ

2 tablespoons olive oil

1 garlic clove, crushed

1 small aubergine, chopped very finely

1 red or ordinary onion, chopped very finely

1 red pepper, de-seeded and sliced

1 large courgette, sliced

125 g (4½ oz) baby corn, halved

125 g (4½ oz) fine green beans, trimmed and halved

3 tomatoes, finely chopped

2 tablespoons sun-dried tomato paste

2 tablespoons red wine vinegar

8 cherry tomatoes, halved

8 stoned black olives, sliced

2 tablespoons chopped fresh parsley

salt and freshly ground black pepper

Enjoy a colourful plate of lightly cooked vegetables in a delicious Greek-style dressing.

1 Heat the olive oil in a frying pan and add the garlic, aubergine and onion, sautéing them over a medium-low heat until very soft – about 10 minutes.

2 Meanwhile, cook the red pepper, courgette, baby corn and green beans in a little boiling water for about 5 minutes, until just tender.

3 Transfer the aubergine mixture to a large bowl and stir in the finely chopped tomatoes and tomato paste. Add the vinegar and season.

4 Drain the simmered vegetables thoroughly, then tip them, while still hot, into the bowl, with the aubergine mixture.

5 Add the halved cherry tomatoes and stir to coat. Leave to cool for about 5 minutes before serving, sprinkled with the black olives and parsley.

Tip… Don't overcook the vegetables; they should retain their crunch and colour.

Fresh tuna Niçoise salad

Serves 1
334 calories per serving

60 g (2 oz) new potatoes,
    halved if large
1 egg
125 g (4½ oz) tuna steak
calorie controlled cooking
    spray
25 g (1 oz) fine green beans
a Little Gem lettuce, leaves
    separated
½ x 400 g can artichokes in
    water, drained
1 tablespoon virtually fat free
    fromage frais
1 teaspoon lemon zest
salt and freshly ground black
    pepper

Fresh tuna is a great way to get your omega 3 fatty acids intake, plus it's quick to cook and very low in fat.

1 Bring a pan of water to the boil, add the potatoes and cook for 10–15 minutes until tender. Hard boil the egg in a separate pan at the same time.

2 Meanwhile, heat a griddle pan or non-stick frying pan until hot. Spray the tuna with the cooking spray and cook for 5–8 minutes (depending on thickness), turning once, until just cooked through. Remove and set aside.

3 Spray the beans with the cooking spray and cook them in the pan used for the tuna, turning occasionally, for 2–3 minutes until tender. Remove from the heat and allow to cool.

4 When the potatoes are ready, drain, refresh in cold water, and drain again. Peel and quarter the egg. Arrange the potatoes on a plate with the beans, lettuce leaves and artichokes. Top with the tuna and egg quarters.

5 Mix together the fromage frais, half the lemon zest and 1 teaspoon of water. Season and then drizzle over the salad, garnishing with the remaining lemon zest.

Tips… If you're making for a packed lunch, keep the dressing in a separate pot until ready to eat, or the salad will wilt.

You could serve this as a warm salad – just keep the potatoes, tuna and green beans warm and serve mixed together with the other ingredients.

Three green bean salad

Serves 2
185 calories per serving
Ⓥ

75 g (2¾ oz) bulgur wheat

50 g (1¾ oz) fine green beans, halved

50 g (1¾ oz) runner beans, trimmed and sliced

100 g (3½ oz) sugar snap peas

a generous pinch of dried chilli flakes

1 tablespoon finely chopped fresh chives

1 tablespoon finely chopped fresh flat leaf parsley

1 tablespoon lemon juice

½ teaspoon granulated artificial sweetener

200 g (7 oz) canned cherry tomatoes in tomato juice

salt and freshly ground black pepper

Green beans and bulgur wheat make a filling lunch or light supper.

1 Bring a pan of water to the boil, add the bulgur wheat and bring it back to the boil. Simmer for 10–15 minutes until tender.

2 Meanwhile, bring another pan of water to the boil. Add the green beans and runner beans and simmer for 2 minutes. Add the sugar snap peas and cook for 1 minute more. Drain and rinse with cold water. Drain again.

3 When the bulgur wheat is tender, drain in a sieve and rinse in cold water until it is cold. Drain again, using the bottom of a bowl to push out the water.

4 Transfer the bulgur wheat to a large bowl and mix in the chilli flakes, fresh chopped herbs, lemon juice, sweetener and cherry tomatoes and juice. Fold through the cooked beans, season and serve.

Creamy mustard potato salad

Serves 1
342 calories per serving
Ⓥ

150 g (5½ oz) new potatoes,
  scrubbed and halved if large
2 teaspoons wholegrain
  mustard
calorie controlled cooking
  spray
2 Quorn Deli Bacon Style
  rashers
1 tablespoon 0% fat Greek
  yogurt
3 cocktail beetroots, halved
a handful of rocket leaves, to
  serve

This potato salad has a lovely, creamy mustard dressing that is especially good with the beetroot and Quorn bacon.

1 Bring a saucepan of water to the boil, add the potatoes and cook for 10–15 minutes until tender. Drain, and while still warm, mix with the mustard. Leave to cool.

2 Lightly coat a non-stick frying pan with the cooking spray and cook the rashers for 2 minutes, turning once, until crispy. Set aside.

3 Mix the yogurt and beetroots into the potatoes. Chop the rashers into small pieces and sprinkle over the top. Serve with the rocket leaves.

Tip… Don't add the rocket leaves until you are ready to serve the salad, otherwise they will wilt.

Bacon and spinach salad

Serves 2

110 calories per serving

200 g packet baby spinach leaves

1 medium slice wholemeal or brown bread, crusts removed

calorie controlled cooking spray

a pinch of dried oregano or thyme

50 g (1¾ oz) lean back bacon, cubed finely

1 tablespoon balsamic vinegar

1 spring onion, sliced into long, thin strips

2 good pinches of sesame seeds

salt and freshly ground black pepper

Take a bag of baby spinach leaves and turn them into a quick, warm salad for a light lunch or starter. The wonderfully crunchy croûtons here are a low fat version of the variety you find in supermarkets and are so tasty.

1 Wash the spinach leaves, if necessary, and dry them thoroughly. Place the leaves in a bowl, cover and set aside.

2 Heat the oven to Gas Mark 6/200°C/fan oven 180°C. Spray the bread slice evenly on both sides with the cooking spray and cut it into small squares. Arrange the squares in a single layer on a baking sheet, season and sprinkle them with the herbs. Bake them for 15 minutes until they are lightly crisp. Remove the baking sheet from the oven and allow the croûtons to cool – they will become even crispier.

3 Heat a non-stick frying pan and spray with the cooking spray. Sauté the bacon, stirring, until it is lightly browned. Stir in the balsamic vinegar and immediately add the spinach and spring onion, tossing it all to make sure the spinach leaves are well coated with the vinegar.

4 Check the seasoning and divide the mixture between two plates. Sprinkle with the sesame seeds and top with the croûtons before serving.

Tip… Make a large batch of croûtons and store them in an airtight container.

Warm Puy lentil salad

Serves 2
274 calories per serving
Ⓥ

Cooked lentils and pulses are a great source of protein for vegetarians. This warm salad is full of contrasting textures and flavours.

80 g (3 oz) Puy lentils, rinsed

125 g (4½ oz) cooked beetroot (not in vinegar)

calorie controlled cooking spray

1½ tablespoons balsamic vinegar

½ teaspoon wholegrain mustard

½ teaspoon walnut oil or extra virgin olive oil

65 g (2¼ oz) mixed salad leaves

6 radishes, halved

50 g (1¾ oz) feta cheese, crumbled

1 Preheat the oven to Gas Mark 6/200°C/fan oven 180°C. Cook the lentils in boiling water for 15–20 minutes until tender but not mushy. Drain and rinse briefly with cold water.

2 Meanwhile, cut the beetroot into wedges. Place in a small roasting tin, coat with the cooking spray and drizzle with ½ a tablespoon of the balsamic vinegar. Roast for 15 minutes or until caramelised around the edges.

3 Whisk the remaining balsamic vinegar with the mustard in a small bowl. Measure out 1 teaspoon of the mixture in a large bowl and whisk in the walnut or olive oil. Toss the salad leaves in the dressing until lightly coated and divide between two bowls or plates. Add the radishes.

4 Mix the rest of the balsamic mixture with the drained lentils and spoon on to the plates. Scatter the roasted beetroot and feta over the salad and serve immediately.

Tips… Nut and seed oils such as walnut oil are strongly flavoured, so a very small amount goes a long way in a salad dressing, yet delivers a big hit in terms of flavour.

If you are cooking for one, the second portion makes a great lunchbox salad, served chilled.

Warm butternut squash and spinach salad

Serves 4
509 calories per serving
Ⓨ

400 g (14 oz) large pasta
  shells
800 g (1 lb 11 oz) butternut
  squash, de-seeded and cut
  into small chunks
100 ml (3½ fl oz) hot vegetable
  stock
125 g (4½ oz) frozen chopped
  spinach
75 g (2¾ oz) reduced fat green
  pesto
50 g (1¾ oz) mild or hot
  Peppadew™ peppers from a
  jar, drained and sliced finely
50 g packet wild rocket
salt and freshly ground black
  pepper

*This salad is delicious hot but can also be served cold –
any leftovers will make the perfect lunchbox filler.*

1 Bring a large pan of water to the boil and cook the pasta for
10–12 minutes, or according to the packet instructions, until al
dente and drain.

2 Meanwhile, put the butternut squash and stock in a wide,
lidded saucepan and bring to the boil. Cover and simmer for
10 minutes, then remove the lid and add the spinach. Cook
for a further 5 minutes, covered, stirring occasionally, until the
spinach is defrosted and warmed through.

3 Drain the pasta and return to the pan. Stir through the
butternut squash and spinach, pesto, peppers and seasoning
for 1–2 minutes until warmed through. Spoon into shallow
bowls and top with the wild rocket. Serve immediately.

Tip… Serve with a 30 g (1¼ oz) slice of garlic bread per
person.

Variation… Try using other squash varieties or pumpkin.

Chicken, turkey and duck

Chicken kebabs

Serves 4
355 calories per serving

400 g (14 oz) skinless,
   boneless chicken breasts,
   cubed
4 red onions, cut into wedges
4 red peppers, de-seeded and
   cut into squares
8 bay leaves
a lemon, cut into wedges
4 medium pitta breads

For the marinade

1 garlic clove, chopped
2 tablespoons low fat natural
   yogurt
1 tablespoon clear honey
1 tablespoon soy sauce
2 tablespoons red wine
   vinegar or lemon juice

*This classic Mediterranean-style recipe can be cooked
either under the grill or on the barbecue.*

1 Preheat the grill to medium. Mix all the marinade ingredients
together in a bowl.

2 Thread the chicken, onions, red peppers, bay leaves and
lemon wedges on to 8 skewers (see Tip).

3 Brush the kebabs with the marinade, reserving a little
to serve them with, and grill for about 10 minutes. Turn
the kebabs at least once, until golden and cooked through.
Meanwhile, warm the pitta breads under the grill.

4 Serve the kebabs in the warmed pitta breads, with the
reserved marinade poured over the top.

Tip… If you are using wooden skewers, soak them in water
for 30 minutes or so before using, to prevent them from
burning.

Variations… Kebabs are great made from pork or beef or
even firm fish like monkfish or scallops.

Try serving the kebabs with couscous instead.

Chicken and potato masala

Serves 4
270 calories per serving
❄

2 onions, sliced thinly

450 g (1 lb) skinless, boneless
  chicken breast, cubed

4 tablespoons medium masala
  curry paste

400 g can chopped tomatoes

200 g (7 oz) mushrooms,
  halved

550 g (1 lb 3 oz) canned new
  potatoes, drained and halved

200 ml (7 fl oz) boiling water

2 tablespoons chopped fresh
  coriander

*Using a ready-prepared curry paste cuts down on
ingredients and the time needed to make this recipe –
and it's delicious.*

1 Dry-fry the onions and chicken in a non-stick pan for
5 minutes. Stir in the curry paste and the tomatoes. Mix well,
and add the mushrooms, potatoes and boiling water. Cover
and simmer for 10 minutes.

2 Stir in the chopped coriander, then serve.

Cumin-spiced chicken

Serves 1
220 calories per serving

calorie controlled cooking spray
½ large onion, sliced
150 g (5½ oz) skinless, boneless chicken breast, cut into 8 pieces
1 garlic clove, crushed
½ teaspoon cumin seeds
½ teaspoon ground coriander
½ teaspoon ground cumin
¼ teaspoon salt
¼ teaspoon turmeric
1 medium green chilli, de-seeded and chopped
150 ml (5 fl oz) chicken stock
1 tablespoon lemon juice
1 tablespoon 0% fat Greek yogurt
salt and freshly ground black pepper

Cumin is an ancient spice, originally from Syria and Egypt. This mildly spiced dish uses both cumin seeds and ground cumin.

1 Heat a non-stick frying pan and spray with the cooking spray. Stir-fry the onion for about 4 minutes until soft.

2 Add the chicken pieces to the pan and continue to cook for 2–3 minutes until they are brown on all sides.

3 Add all the other ingredients, except the lemon juice and yogurt. Heat gently until simmering, then cover the pan with a tight-fitting lid and cook for 15 minutes.

4 Remove the lid and cook for 2–3 minutes longer until the sauce has reduced and thickened.

5 Stir in the lemon juice and yogurt, season to taste, then serve.

Tip... Serve with steamed broccoli and garnish with some chopped red chilli for an extra spicy kick.

Jambalaya

Serves 1
400 calories per serving

50 g (1¾ oz) dried long grain
rice
calorie controlled cooking
spray
1 celery stick, sliced
3 spring onions, chopped
½ small green pepper,
de-seeded and chopped
1 small garlic clove, crushed
½ teaspoon Cajun spice mix,
or according to taste
½ teaspoon fresh thyme
leaves or ¼ teaspoon dried
thyme
15 g (½ oz) chorizo sausage,
sliced
1 tomato, chopped
50 g (1¾ oz) skinless,
boneless, cooked chicken,
chopped
50 g (1¾ oz) large peeled
prawns, defrosted if frozen
salt and freshly ground black
pepper
fresh thyme sprigs, to garnish

*This easy and delicious Cajun dish from the Deep South of
the USA was influenced by the flavours of Spain.*

1 Cook the rice in plenty of boiling water for about 12 minutes
until tender.

2 Meanwhile, heat a large frying pan or wok and lightly spray
with the cooking spray. Add the celery, spring onions, green
pepper and garlic. Sauté them for about 3 minutes, until
softened.

3 Add the Cajun seasoning, thyme, chorizo, tomato and
chicken. Cook gently, stirring occasionally, for a further
5 minutes.

4 Drain the rice thoroughly and add it to the frying pan, stirring
well to combine everything. Add the prawns and cook for
another 2–3 minutes, until they are heated through. Season
with salt and pepper and serve, garnished with sprigs of thyme.

Tip… If you can't find Cajun spice mix, use 1 teaspoon of
mild chilli powder and a pinch of cayenne pepper, adding
more or less according to taste.

Variation… Omit the sausage and chicken, and add another
50 g (1¾ oz) of prawns.

Chicken korma

Serves 1
350 calories per serving

calorie controlled cooking
   spray
1 onion, sliced thinly
150 g (5½ oz) skinless,
   boneless chicken breast,
   cubed
1 garlic clove, crushed
2.5 cm (1 inch) fresh root
   ginger, peeled and grated
½ cinnamon stick
2 cardamom pods, crushed
   slightly
½ teaspoon cumin seeds
½ teaspoon mild chilli powder
½ teaspoon ground turmeric
50 g (1¾ oz) 0% fat Greek
   yogurt
100 g (3½ oz) low fat plain bio
   yogurt
1 tablespoon ground almonds
3 tablespoons skimmed milk
salt and freshly ground black
   pepper

*This is a mild, creamy curry that is good served with
steamed green beans, mixed with a little chopped tomato
and an Indian bread, such as naan, to soak up the sauce.*

1 Heat a lidded, non-stick frying pan and spray with the
cooking spray. Stir-fry the onion for about 5 minutes until soft.

2 Add the chicken pieces to the pan and cook for 5 minutes or
until brown on all sides.

3 Add the rest of the ingredients, except the skimmed milk.
Heat the mixture gently until it is simmering, then cover the
pan with the lid and cook for 15 minutes.

4 Remove the lid and cook for a few minutes more to
concentrate the flavour of the sauce; then add the skimmed
milk and stir well.

5 Season the korma to taste and serve.

Chicken chow mein

Serves 4
420 calories per serving

300 g (10½ oz) egg noodles
1 teaspoon sesame oil
calorie controlled cooking
   spray
4 spring onions, sliced finely
1 tablespoon oyster sauce
200 g (7 oz) chicken mince
400 g (14 oz) Savoy cabbage,
   shredded thinly
150 g (5½ oz) oyster, shiitake
   or button mushrooms, sliced
   thinly
2 medium carrots, cut into
   matchsticks
125 ml (4 fl oz) hot chicken
   stock
2 tablespoons soy sauce

*Forget ordering a Chinese take-away and rustle up this
quick and easy chicken noodle dish.*

1 Cook the noodles according to the packet instructions, drain
and toss with the sesame oil.

2 Heat a wok or large frying-pan and spray with the cooking
spray. Stir-fry the spring onions, oyster sauce and mince for
3–4 minutes.

3 Add the cabbage, mushrooms, carrots and stock, cover and
simmer for 3–4 minutes, or until the carrots are just tender.
Uncover and cook for 3 minutes more, or until the liquid has
evaporated.

4 Stir in the soy sauce, add the noodles and stir-fry until
heated through. Serve immediately.

Variations... Try using spinach, peas, bamboo shoots or
beansprouts. Any fish or meat can be used; for example,
pork or turkey mince, or raw, shelled prawns.

Sweet and sour chicken with noodles

Serves 4
375 calories per serving

175 g (6 oz) instant noodles

2 tablespoons light soy sauce

2 tablespoons rice, white wine or cider vinegar

2 tablespoons sherry

2 teaspoons light muscovado sugar

1 tablespoon cornflour

1 teaspoon Chinese five spice

210 g can pineapple chunks in natural juice

1 tablespoon stir-fry oil or vegetable oil

350 g (12 oz) chicken stir-fry strips

1 onion, finely sliced

1 large carrot, finely sliced

1 courgette, finely sliced

3 tomatoes, de-seeded and chopped

salt and freshly ground black pepper

fresh coriander or flat leaf parsley, to garnish (optional)

Stir-fried strips of chicken taste fabulous in this quick and easy dish that the whole family will enjoy.

1 Soak the noodles in boiling water for 6 minutes, or follow the packet instructions.

2 Mix together the soy sauce, vinegar, sherry, sugar, cornflour and five spice powder. Drain the pineapple, adding the juice to the soy sauce mixture. Set aside.

3 Heat the oil in a wok or a very large non-stick frying-pan. Add the chicken, a handful at a time, and stir-fry over a high heat for 3–4 minutes.

4 Add the onion, carrot and courgette to the chicken. Stir-fry for another 3–4 minutes, then add the tomatoes and pineapple chunks. Stir the soy sauce mixture and add to the chicken and vegetables, stirring until hot and thickened. Season to taste.

5 Drain the noodles and divide between 4 warm plates. Pile the stir-fry on top, then serve, garnished with fresh coriander or parsley, if using.

Variation… For speed and convenience, use a bag of ready-prepared stir-fry vegetables, either fresh or frozen.

Leftover turkey patties

Serves 4
265 calories per serving

450 g (1 lb) potatoes, cut into equal-size pieces

175 g (6 oz) cooked Brussels sprouts or winter greens, shredded

175 g (6 oz) cooked turkey meat, cubed

75 g (2¾ oz) cooked ham, cubed

2 tablespoons seasoned flour

1 tablespoon vegetable oil

salt and freshly ground black pepper

Here is a well-known and tasty way of using up leftovers. Serve the patties with pickles and extra vegetables or a tomato and basil salad.

1 Cook the potatoes in lightly salted boiling water for 15–20 minutes until tender. Drain and mash.

2 Mix the vegetables, turkey and ham into the mash. Season and shape into 8 patties. Dust in the seasoned flour.

3 Heat half the oil in a large non-stick frying pan and fry the patties for 4–5 minutes on each side until golden brown. Do this in two batches, using the remaining oil, as required. Drain the cooked patties on kitchen paper before serving.

Turkey and apple burgers

Serves 4
196 calories per serving

1 small onion, grated
1 apple, cored and grated
1 teaspoon dried thyme
450 g (1 lb) lean turkey mince
1 small egg, lightly beaten
2 tablespoons plain flour, for
  dusting
calorie controlled cooking
  spray
salt and freshly ground black
  pepper

*If you have time, these succulent burgers benefit from
chilling for 30 minutes before cooking.*

1 Put the onion, apple, thyme and turkey mince in a bowl and
mix together. Add the egg and seasoning, then mix again.

2 Lightly dust a plate with the flour. Using wet hands, divide
the mince mixture into four and shape each portion into a
round, flat burger. Place on the plate and, using dry hands, turn
and lightly dust them in the flour.

3 Spray a griddle pan or non-stick frying pan with the cooking
spray, place the burgers in the pan, then spray again. Fry for
about 8 minutes on each side until cooked through and golden.
Serve immediately.

Tip… Serve in a 50 g (1¾ oz) toasted wholemeal bun with
lettuce, tomato, red onion, cress and grated carrot.

Chinese turkey skewers with noodles

Serves 4
405 calories per serving

3 tablespoons soy sauce
1 tablespoon tomato purée
1 teaspoon sweet chilli sauce
2 teaspoons caster sugar
150 ml (5 fl oz) hot chicken stock
450 g (1 lb) skinless, boneless turkey breast fillets, cut into strips lengthways
250 g packet medium egg noodles
½ a Chinese cabbage, shredded
100 g (3½ oz) baby corn or asparagus tips, trimmed

Spicy kebabs served on a filling plateful of vegetables and noodles.

1 Preheat the grill to high. Mix together the soy sauce, tomato purée, chilli sauce and sugar. Put half of this into a small pan with the stock. Add the turkey to the remaining sauce, and coat well. Thread the turkey on to four skewers (see Tip, page 36) and grill for 6–8 minutes, turning occasionally, until cooked.

2 Meanwhile, break the noodles into a large pan of boiling water. Add the cabbage and baby corn or asparagus tips. Bring to the boil, cover and simmer for 4 minutes.

3 Heat through the sauce in the pan.

4 Drain the noodles and vegetables, then return them to the pan, pour on the warmed sauce and toss to coat thoroughly. Divide between four plates and serve with a kebab on top.

Cantonese orange duck

Serves 2
244 calories per serving

1 tablespoon sweet chilli sauce

6 tablespoons fresh orange juice

1 tablespoon light soy sauce

240 g (8½ oz) skinless duck breast, cut into 1 cm (½ inch) slices

calorie controlled cooking spray

2 spring onions, sliced diagonally

2 cm (¾ inch) fresh root ginger, sliced into thin rounds

½ teaspoon Chinese five spice

a small orange, peeled and cut into thin rounds

salt and freshly ground black pepper

A fabulous flavour-packed way to cook duck breast.

1 Mix together the sweet chilli sauce, orange juice and soy sauce.

2 Heat a wok or large non-stick frying pan. Spray the duck with the cooking spray, then stir-fry for 3 minutes. Add the white part of the spring onions and ginger, then stir-fry for another 2 minutes.

3 Add the soy sauce mixture to the pan with the Chinese five spice and stir-fry for 2 minutes. Add the orange and cook for 1 minute until reduced and thickened. Season and scatter over the green part of the spring onion before serving.

Tips… For an extra kick, add a pinch of chilli flakes in step 3 with the soy sauce.

Serve with 50 g (1¾ oz) dried brown basmati rice per person, cooked according to the packet instructions.

Variation… Swap the duck for 250 g (9 oz) lean pork strips and cook for the same length of time.

Turkey tagliatelle with asparagus and peas

Serves 4

435 calories per serving

225 g (8 oz) dried tagliatelle or spaghetti

2 teaspoons olive oil

225 g (8 oz) turkey stir-fry strips

a bunch of spring onions, trimmed and finely chopped

100 g (3½ oz) asparagus spears, trimmed and chopped

100 g (3½ oz) frozen petits pois or garden peas

200 g (7 oz) virtually fat free fromage frais

200 g (7 oz) low fat soft cheese with garlic and herbs

salt and freshly ground black pepper

a few basil leaves, to garnish

Low fat soft cheese makes a lovely creamy sauce stirred into warm pasta.

1 Cook the tagliatelle or spaghetti in plenty of boiling water for about 8–10 minutes, until just tender.

2 Meanwhile, heat the olive oil in a large saucepan and sauté the turkey strips for about 5–6 minutes, until golden. Add the spring onions and cook for another 2–3 minutes, then add the asparagus and frozen peas. Cook, stirring, for 2–3 minutes.

3 Add the fromage frais, soft cheese and most of the basil leaves to the saucepan. Heat, stirring gently, for about 3 minutes until melted and blended. Season with salt and pepper.

4 Drain the pasta well. Add it to the sauce and stir gently to mix. Transfer to four warm plates and serve at once, garnished with basil leaves.

Variations… Use chicken stir-fry strips instead of turkey, if you prefer.

If asparagus is out of season or very expensive, use fine green beans instead.

Cajun turkey with sweet potato mash

Serves 4
270 calories per serving

juice of a lime
2 teaspoons Cajun spice mix
4 x 150 g (5½ oz) skinless, boneless turkey breast portions
calorie controlled cooking spray
500 g (1 lb 2 oz) sweet potato, cubed
2 tablespoons chopped fresh coriander
salt and freshly ground black pepper

Sweet potato makes a nice change from ordinary mash.

1 In a bowl, mix together the lime juice and Cajun spice mix. Add the turkey breast portions, coat well in the marinade and leave for 5 minutes.

2 Meanwhile, bring a saucepan of water to the boil, add the sweet potato and cook for 10 minutes or until tender. Drain, return the potatoes to the pan and mash until smooth. Season well.

3 Heat a non-stick griddle pan. Remove the turkey from the marinade, spray with the cooking spray and cook for about 5 minutes on each side until cooked through. Serve with the sweet potato mash and sprinkle with the coriander.

Tip... Serve with 100 g (3½ oz) sugar snap peas per person.

Plum duck with watercress

Serves 2
187 calories per serving

2 tablespoons Chinese plum
sauce
1 tablespoon soy sauce
1 cm (½ inch) fresh root
ginger, chopped finely
1 garlic clove, sliced
calorie controlled cooking
spray
150 g (5½ oz) skinless duck
breast fillet, sliced thinly
2 carrots, halved and sliced
thinly on the diagonal
1 celery stick, sliced thinly
1 red onion, chopped
a handful of watercress
freshly ground black pepper

*The secret to a good stir-fry is to have all the ingredients
prepared before you start cooking.*

1 In a bowl, mix the plum sauce and soy sauce with 3
tablespoons of water. Add the ginger and garlic then set aside.

2 Heat a lidded wok or large non-stick frying pan and spray
with the cooking spray. Add the duck, season with black pepper
and cook very briefly, until the it just turns brown. Remove from
the pan and set aside.

3 Add the carrots, celery and onion to the pan, add a
little water, then cover and steam fry for 5 minutes so the
vegetables soften, but still have a little bite.

4 Pour in the plum sauce mixture and allow it to bubble then
toss in the duck and watercress. Serve immediately.

Tips... Serve with 60 g (2 oz) dried rice per person, cooked
according to the packet instructions.

When using salty ingredients such as soy sauce, there is
no need to add salt when seasoning.

Speedy turkey meatballs

Serves 4
208 calories per serving
❄

1 onion
calorie controlled cooking
   spray
200 g (7 oz) mushrooms,
   chopped roughly
salt and freshly ground black
   pepper
300 ml (10 fl oz) chicken stock
2 wholewheat crispbreads,
   crushed (see Tip)
500 g (1 lb 2 oz) turkey mince
400 g can chopped tomatoes

*Serve the meatballs with some lightly cooked green
vegetables such as broccoli and green beans.*

1 Chop half the onion and fry in the cooking spray in
a medium pan for 2 minutes. Stir in the mushrooms, seasoning
and 3 tablespoons of the stock. Cover the pan and cook for
2 minutes.

2 Meanwhile, grate the remaining onion into a bowl, add the
crispbread crumbs and moisten with 2 tablespoons of stock.
Mix in the turkey mince and seasoning and shape into 20
meatballs.

3 Add the tomatoes and the rest of the stock to the onion and
mushroom mixture. Season and simmer the sauce for about
5 minutes.

4 Meanwhile, brown the meatballs in the cooking spray in
a non-stick frying pan for 5 minutes, turning to colour them
evenly. Add them to the sauce and simmer, uncovered, for
15 minutes, until cooked through.

Tip... Crush the crispbreads in a plastic bag on your
chopping board, using the can of tomatoes.

Beef, lamb and pork

Beef tataki

Serves 2

262 calories per serving

100 g (3½ oz) Little Gem lettuce, shredded

30 g (1¼ oz) pea shoots

½ small red onion, sliced thinly into rings

2.5 cm (1 inch) cucumber, quartered, de-seeded and sliced thinly

4 radishes, sliced thinly into rounds

2 x 150 g (5½ oz) lean beef fillet steaks

calorie controlled cooking spray

For the dressing

1 tablespoon light soy sauce

1 tablespoon lime juice

½ teaspoon caster sugar

1 teaspoon grated fresh root ginger

salt and freshly ground black pepper

In Japanese, the word 'tataki' means 'to sear on the outside'. In this recipe, the steaks are seared on the barbecue or cooked under the grill.

1 Light the barbecue or preheat the grill to high. Mix together the ingredients for the dressing and season with black pepper. Arrange the lettuce and pea shoots on 2 serving plates, then top with the red onion, cucumber and radishes.

2 Spray the steaks with the cooking spray and season. Barbecue them over a high heat or cook under the grill for about 1–2 minutes on each side or until cooked to your liking. Remove from the heat, then leave to rest, covered, for 5 minutes.

3 Slice each steak across the grain and arrange them on top of the salad. Drizzle the dressing over the top.

Japanese-style fondue

Serves 4
439 calories per serving

400 g (14 oz) rump steak
250 g (9 oz) tofu
250 g (9 oz) shiitake
  mushrooms
calorie controlled cooking
  spray
a bunch of spring onions,
  chopped
200 ml (7 fl oz) sukiyaki sauce
300 ml (10 fl oz) beef stock
125 ml (4 fl oz) boiling water
100 g (3½ oz) mange tout,
  halved
75 g (2¾ oz) canned bamboo
  shoots, drained
225 g (8 oz) baby spinach
  leaves
2 x 150 g packets of ready-
  cooked udon noodles

Ideally, people will sit round the table and cook their own food, fondue style, for this dish. An electric wok or a fondue set with a large bowl is ideal.

1 Trim and discard any fat from the steak and cut it into thin strips. Cut the tofu into bite size rectangles. Place both on a large plate.

2 Remove the stalks from the mushrooms (but do not discard them) and cut a cross into the cap of the mushrooms to help them cook.

3 Heat the wok or fondue bowl and spray with the cooking spray. Gently fry the spring onions for 2 minutes. Add the sukiyaki sauce, stock and boiling water. Bring to a gentle simmer.

4 Add half the vegetables (including the mushroom stalks) and noodles and simmer gently for 5 minutes. Then let each person cook some meat and tofu in the simmering stock, using wooden skewers or fondue forks. Once cooked to taste, they can transfer it to their bowls with some vegetables and noodles.

5 When half the meat has been used up, add the rest of the vegetables and simmer as in step 4. To finish, pour the remaining enriched stock into everyone's bowls and serve it as a soup.

Tip… If you don't have a fondue set or electric wok, use a wok on the hob and cook the food in stages.

☻ **Variation…** Add another 250 g (9 oz) tofu to replace the beef and use vegetable stock.

Peppered beef steak with creamy mushroom sauce

Serves 4
215 calories per serving

1 teaspoon peppercorns
1 teaspoon coriander seeds
4 x 110 g (4 oz) fillet steaks at room temperature

For the sauce
calorie controlled cooking spray
350 g (12 oz) mushrooms, chopped roughly
2 garlic cloves
200 ml (7 fl oz) hot beef stock
60 g (2 oz) low fat soft cheese
1 tablespoon cornflour
1 teaspoon lemon juice
2 tablespoons snipped fresh chives

Sugar snap peas go really well with these steaks in a rich sauce.

1 Crush the peppercorns and coriander seeds in a pestle and mortar and press on to both sides of the steaks. Set aside.

2 Heat a large, lidded saucepan until hot and spray with the cooking spray. Add the mushrooms and cook for 1 minute, then add the garlic and 2 tablespoons of the stock. Cover and cook for 5 minutes. Stir in the soft cheese, followed by the remaining stock, and bring to a simmer.

3 Blend the cornflour with a little cold water, then add to the mushroom sauce and stir until thickened. Add the lemon juice, stir in the chives and keep warm.

4 To cook the steaks, heat a large non-stick frying pan until hot and spray with the cooking spray. Fry the steaks for 1½ minutes on each side over a high heat to brown, then reduce the heat to medium. Cook them for a further 3 minutes on each side for medium rare and 5 minutes on each side for well done. Rest the steaks for a couple of minutes before serving with the mushroom sauce spooned over.

Tips… Low fat soft cheese is very versatile – use it to add richness to sauces, toss it through pasta or simply enjoy it as a spread.

Stir-fried beef noodles

Serves 2
445 calories per serving

100 g (3½ oz) medium rice
noodles
calorie controlled cooking
spray
½ small red onion, sliced
1 red chilli, de-seeded and
cubed
2 garlic cloves, sliced
2 x 110 g (4 oz) lean fillet
steak, sliced finely
½ red pepper, de-seeded and
sliced finely
125 g (4½ oz) mange tout
juice of 2 limes
2 tablespoons Thai fish sauce
1 teaspoon lemongrass purée
(oil free)
1 egg, beaten
2 spring onions, sliced finely
2 tablespoons chopped fresh
coriander

This classic noodle dish is so quick and easy to make.

1 Cook the noodles in boiling water according to the packet
instructions. Drain and rinse in cold water. Set aside.

2 Heat a wok until hot. Spray with the cooking spray. Stir-fry
the onion, chilli and garlic for 2–3 minutes. Add the steak.
Stir-fry for 1 minute, stirring constantly. Add the pepper and
mange tout. Cook for 2 minutes.

3 Pour in the lime juice, fish sauce and lemongrass purée.
Let the mixture bubble for a few seconds, then toss through
the cooked noodles.

4 Pour in the beaten egg and allow the mixture to set for
1 minute. Quickly stir to shred the egg and serve scattered
with the spring onions and coriander.

Greek meat patties

Serves 4
350 calories per serving
✳ (uncooked patties)

6 medium slices bread, crusts removed
1 onion, chopped finely
a bunch of flat leaf parsley, chopped finely
a bunch of mint, chopped finely
2 eggs
zest and juice of ½ a lemon
300 g (10½ oz) lamb mince
70 g (2½ oz) plain flour
calorie controlled cooking spray
salt and freshly ground black pepper

These patties – keftethes *in Greek – are delicious served with rice and salad.*

1 Soak the bread in a few tablespoons of water and then squeeze it dry with your hands. Put the bread in a bowl with all the other ingredients except the flour and cooking spray. Mix to a paste.

2 With moistened hands, shape the mixture into 12 burger-shaped patties. Put the flour in a shallow tray and coat the patties in it.

3 Spray a large non-stick frying pan with the cooking spray and fry the patties in 2 batches for 5 minutes on each side until thoroughly cooked through. Drain them on kitchen paper before serving.

Variations… Make the patties smaller and serve as a starter or cocktail nibble.

Although they won't be authentically Greek, try making these patties with turkey mince for a delicious, low fat version.

Steak, mushrooms and sweet potato chips

Serves 4

426 calories per serving

800 g (1 lb 11 oz) sweet
  potatoes, cut into chunky
  chips
calorie controlled cooking
  spray
4 large flat mushrooms
300 g (10½ oz) leeks, trimmed
  and sliced
125 g (4½ oz) low fat soft
  cheese with garlic and herbs
4 x 110 g (4 oz) lean beef
  medallion steaks
salt and freshly ground black
  pepper

*Tender juicy steaks served with stuffed mushrooms and
a new twist on oven chips.*

1 Preheat the oven to Gas Mark 7/220°C/fan oven 200°C.

2 Lightly spray the sweet potato chips with the cooking spray
and spread out on a baking tray. Place it on a high oven shelf
and cook for 25 minutes, turning the chips halfway through.

3 Once the sweet potatoes are in the oven, remove the stalks
from the mushrooms and set the stalks aside. Season the
mushrooms and place them, open cup side up, in a roasting tin.
Spray with the cooking spray, cover with foil and bake below
the potatoes for 7 minutes until tender.

4 Meanwhile, to make the filling, chop the mushroom stalks.
Spray a lidded, non-stick saucepan with the cooking spray.
Add the leeks and stalks with 3 tablespoons of water and cook,
covered, for 3 minutes until softened. Stir in the low fat soft
cheese. Take the mushrooms out of the oven, remove the foil
and spoon in the filling. Return the uncovered mushrooms to
the oven for 10 minutes until lightly browned.

5 Meanwhile, spray a non-stick frying pan with the cooking
spray. Cook the steaks for 3–4 minutes on each side, or until
cooked to your liking. Serve with the stuffed mushrooms and
sweet potato chips.

Ⓥ **Variation…** Double the quantity of leeks and soft cheese
and the number of mushrooms to replace the beef. Serve
two stuffed mushrooms per person with the chips.

Speedy shepherd's pie

Serves 4
355 calories per serving
❄

500 g (1 lb 2 oz) large
 potatoes, peeled and cubed
5 tablespoons semi-skimmed
 milk
450 g (1 lb) extra lean beef
 mince
150 ml (5 fl oz) hot beef stock
300 ml pot low fat fresh
 tomato pasta sauce
2 teaspoons Worcestershire
 sauce
salt and freshly ground black
 pepper

This is a foolproof way of ensuring the family get to the
table on time. Serve with broccoli or courgettes.

1 Cook the potatoes in boiling water for 12–15 minutes or until
tender. Drain and mash with the milk and salt and pepper, to
taste. Preheat the grill to medium.

2 Meanwhile, dry-fry the beef mince in a large non-stick
saucepan for 5 minutes. Stir in the stock, pasta sauce and
Worcestershire sauce. Simmer gently for 10 minutes until the
mince is tender. Season to taste.

3 Spoon the mince into a shallow 1.2 litre (2 pint) flameproof
dish and top evenly with the mashed potato. Place under the
grill for 4–5 minutes, or until the topping is golden brown.

Tip... You could try adding 2 grated carrots or 125 g
(4½ oz) frozen peas to the pasta sauce in step 2.

Lamb stew with flame-roasted peppers and olives

Serves 2
461 calories per serving
❄

2 x 125 g (4½ oz) lean lamb steaks, trimmed of visible fat
calorie controlled cooking spray
1 onion, sliced
100 g (3½ oz) fennel, sliced into wedges
2 garlic cloves, sliced thinly
200 ml (7 fl oz) dry white wine
4 fresh thyme sprigs
200 ml (7 fl oz) vegetable stock
50 g (1¾ oz) green olives in brine, drained
100 g (3½ oz) flame-roasted red peppers from a jar, drained and torn into pieces
salt and freshly ground black pepper

A speedy Mediterranean stew for two.

1 Heat a deep, lidded, non-stick frying pan. Spray the lamb steaks with the cooking spray and season. Cook the lamb for 2 minutes on each side until browned, then remove, cover and set aside.

2 Add the onion and fennel to the pan, spray with the cooking spray, and sauté for 5 minutes until softened. Stir in the garlic and cook for a minute before pouring in the wine and adding the thyme sprigs. Allow the wine to bubble and reduce for about 5 minutes.

3 Add the stock, olives and peppers and bring to the boil. Reduce the heat and simmer, partially covered, for 5 minutes. Return the lamb to the pan, spoon the juices over the top, cover and simmer for another 5 minutes until the meat is tender and the vegetables are cooked. Season and serve.

Tips… Soak up the juices with some delicious mashed potato. For two people, cook 200 g (7 oz) cubed potatoes for 10 minutes or until tender. Drain and mash with 2 tablespoons of extra light mayonnaise and 50 ml (2 fl oz) skimmed milk until creamy. Season before serving.

Ready-prepared flame-roasted red peppers can be bought in jars and will keep in the fridge for a couple of weeks after opening.

Jerk lamb

Serves 4
308 calories per serving

2 x 250 g (9 oz) racks of lamb,
  fat removed
calorie controlled cooking
  spray
1 tablespoon jerk seasoning
zest and juice of ½ a lime
25 g packet fresh coriander
3 x 15 g (½ oz) wholewheat
  crispbreads, broken
2 teaspoons tomato purée
salt

*Caribbean jerk seasoning can turn rack of lamb into an
exotic supper dish.*

1 Preheat the oven to Gas Mark 6/200°C/fan oven 180°C and
put a baking tray in the oven to heat. Heat a non-stick frying
pan until hot and spray the lamb racks with the cooking spray.
Fry the lamb racks for 5 minutes until brown all over. Set aside.

2 In a food processor, whizz together the jerk seasoning, lime
zest and juice, coriander and crispbreads. Season with salt.
Brush the back of each lamb rack with the tomato purée and
gently press the spicy crispbread crumbs on to the lamb.

3 Remove the baking tray from the oven and transfer the lamb
to the baking tray, crust upwards. Roast the racks in the oven
for 20 minutes or until cooked to your liking. Carve into cutlets
and serve immediately.

Tip... Serve with 60 g (2 oz) mashed potato (made with
1 tablespoon skimmed milk) per person, cooked asparagus
and baby carrots.

Rosemary lamb fillets

Serves 2
182 calories per serving
❄

The delicious smell that fills the house while this dish cooks will have everyone queuing up in the kitchen! Serve with minted peas and whole, steamed carrots.

1 teaspoon ground cumin

8 rosemary sprigs, tough stems removed, leaves chopped finely

1 teaspoon olive oil

2 x 90 g (3¼ oz) lamb fillets

calorie controlled cooking spray

2 red onions, cut into thin wedges

3 tablespoons balsamic vinegar

salt and freshly ground black pepper

1 Mix the cumin, rosemary and seasoning together on a plate. Rub the olive oil into the lamb fillets and roll them in the seasoned mixture until covered.

2 Heat a frying pan and gently fry the fillets for 12–15 minutes, turning occasionally, or until cooked through. Remove from the pan to a carving board, cover with foil and leave to rest for a few minutes.

3 Meanwhile, spray the pan with the cooking spray and add the onions. Stir-fry for 10 minutes, adding a little water if they stick, until softened. Then add the balsamic vinegar and seasoning and stir-fry for a further 3–5 minutes. Serve the onions as an accompaniment to the lamb.

Sausage and red pepper bake

Serves 4
311 calories per serving

This family meal is a great way to sneak extra vegetables past the kids by mixing them with sausages.

calorie controlled cooking spray
454 g packet reduced fat Cumberland sausages
1 red onion, cubed
2 red peppers, de-seeded and cubed
1 courgette, trimmed and cubed
1 tablespoon dried thyme
2 tablespoons balsamic vinegar
400 g can chopped tomatoes
4 x 26 g ready-made garlic bread slices
salt and freshly ground black pepper

1 Preheat the oven to Gas Mark 6/200°C/fan oven 180°C. Put a roasting tin on the hob and spray with the cooking spray. Add the sausages and cook for 2 minutes, turning until lightly browned. Remove from the heat and stir in the onion, red peppers, courgette, thyme, balsamic vinegar and seasoning. Spray again with the cooking spray and bake in the oven for 15 minutes.

2 Stir in the chopped tomatoes, then top with the garlic bread and bake in the oven for a further 10 minutes until golden. Serve immediately.

Tip... 100 g (3½ oz) cooked potatoes mashed with 1 tablespoon of skimmed milk per person and steamed green beans are the ideal side dishes for this bake.

🅥 **Variation...** Use 8 x 50 g (1¾ oz) Quorn Sausages instead.

Hot sticky sausages

Serves 4
313 calories per serving

400 g (14 oz) floury potatoes, cut into medium sized chunks

calorie controlled cooking spray

8 Weight Watchers Premium Pork Sausages

1 tablespoon low fat spread

½ x 25 g packet fresh coriander, chopped finely

salt and freshly ground black pepper

For the glaze

½ teaspoon English mustard powder

½ teaspoon ground allspice

juice of ½ an orange

2 tablespoons clear honey

a generous pinch of cayenne pepper

Transform traditional bangers and mash into gourmet cuisine.

1 Bring a medium pan of water to the boil, add the potatoes, cover and simmer for 15 minutes until tender.

2 Meanwhile, to make the glaze, mix together the mustard powder, allspice, orange juice, honey and cayenne pepper in a small bowl.

3 Heat a non-stick frying pan and spray with the cooking spray. Gently cook the sausages for 15 minutes, turning until cooked. Drizzle the glaze over the sausages and turn to coat. Bubble the glaze for 3 minutes until sticky and the sausages are coated. Keep them warm.

4 Drain the potatoes and return to the pan. Mash the potatoes with the low fat spread until smooth. Stir in the coriander and season to taste. Serve immediately with the sausages.

Tip... Serve with griddled courgettes, cherry tomatoes and red pepper.

Ⓥ **Variation...** Instead of the pork sausages use 8 x 50 g (1¾ oz) Quorn Sausages instead.

Bangers and mash with onion gravy

Serves 2
404 calories per serving

1 onion, sliced thickly
4 Weight Watchers Premium Pork Sausages
1 teaspoon olive oil
500 g (1 lb 2 oz) potatoes, peeled and cubed
5 tablespoons skimmed milk
freshly grated nutmeg, to taste
1 tablespoon cornflour
150 ml (5 fl oz) vegetable stock
1 tablespoon tomato ketchup
salt and freshly ground black pepper

A family favourite served with sweet roasted onion gravy.

1 Preheat the oven to Gas Mark 6/200°C/fan oven 180°C. Toss the onion and sausages with the oil and seasoning and spread out on a baking tray. Roast in the oven for 10 minutes, then turn the sausages over and stir the onions around. Return to the oven for 5 minutes, then remove the roasted onions to a plate and cook the sausages for a further 5 minutes.

2 As soon as the sausages and onions go in the oven, add the potatoes to a large pan of boiling water. Cook for about 15 minutes or until tender, then drain.

3 Heat the milk in the pan, add the drained potatoes and mash together. Add nutmeg and seasoning to taste.

4 While the potatoes are cooking, blend the cornflour with a little of the stock in a non-stick saucepan, to make a paste. Mix in the remaining stock and ketchup and simmer for 5 minutes, then add the roasted onions and simmer for a further 2 minutes. Pour the onion gravy over the bangers and mash to serve.

Pork skewers with rouille sauce

Serves 4
275 calories per serving

This red sauce from Provence is the ideal spicy, smoky accompaniment to pork.

300 g (10½ oz) baby new
  potatoes, halved
1 medium slice bread, cubed
a pinch of saffron threads
175 g (6 oz) flame-roasted red
  peppers from a jar, drained
  and chopped roughly
½ teaspoon smoked paprika
1 garlic clove, chopped
4 x 150 g (5½ oz) lean pork
  loin steaks, visible fat
  removed and cubed
2 large red onions, cut into
  8 wedges
calorie controlled cooking
  spray

1 Bring a medium pan of water to the boil, add the potatoes, cover and simmer for 10 minutes until nearly tender.

2 Meanwhile, put the bread into a bowl and sprinkle with the saffron and 6 tablespoons hot water from the tap. Set aside. Drain the potatoes and plunge into cold water. Drain again.

3 To make the rouille sauce, put the peppers, paprika and garlic into a food processor and whizz until finely minced. Add the soaked bread and any leftover juices and whizz again until smooth.

4 Preheat the grill to medium hot. Thread the pork, onion and potatoes on to 8 metal skewers and spray with the cooking spray. Cook under the grill for 10 minutes, turning until cooked. Serve with the rouille sauce on the side as a dip.

Tip... Serve with a generous mixed salad, drizzled with 1 tablespoon fat free salad dressing, and a warm mini pitta bread per person.

Pork and piccalilli escalopes with apple mash

Serves 2
310 calories per serving

1 large potato, about 275 g
  (9½ oz), sliced thinly
1 small Bramley apple
2 x 100 g (3½ oz) pork steaks
2 tablespoons piccalilli
1 teaspoon chopped fresh
  chives
salt and freshly ground black
  pepper

*Piccalilli is a vivid crunchy vegetable relish that goes
well with pork. The potato and apple mash is a delicious
variation.*

1 Cook the potato slices in boiling water for 10 minutes until
tender. Peel the apple and slice it into the pan. Cover the
saucepan and leave to stand for 5 minutes.

2 Meanwhile dry-fry the pork for 3 minutes on each side. Add
the piccalilli and 4 tablespoons of water. Stir briskly to blend
the ingredients. Season to taste.

3 Drain and crush the potatoes and apple. Stir in the chives
and season to taste. Serve the pork and piccalilli pan juices
with the mash.

Tip... Always look for lean cuts of pork such as stir-fry
strips, steaks, escalopes and fillet.

Glazed pork chops with mushroom ragù

Serves 2

270 calories per serving

1 tablespoon clear honey

1 tablespoon wholegrain mustard

4 x 75 g (2¾ oz) lean pork chops, fat removed

For the ragù

calorie controlled cooking spray

1 garlic clove, crushed

200 g (7 oz) mushrooms, chopped

400 g can chopped tomatoes

½ teaspoon dried herbes de Provence or oregano

a small bunch of basil or flat leaf parsley, chopped (optional)

salt and freshly ground black pepper

These tender pork chops are brushed with a honey and wholegrain mustard glaze and served with a tangy mushroom and tomato ragù.

1 First make the ragù. Heat a large frying pan and spray with the cooking spray, then fry the garlic for 1 minute. Add the mushrooms and stir-fry on a high heat for 5 minutes.

2 Add the tomatoes and dried herbs. Bring to the boil and simmer gently, uncovered, for 10–15 minutes or until thick. Taste and season and stir through the fresh herbs, if using, before serving.

3 Preheat the grill. Gently heat the honey and mustard together in a small saucepan and brush this glaze over the pork chops. Grill the chops on one side for 3–4 minutes.

4 Turn them over, brush again with the glaze and grill the other side for a few minutes or until the chops are golden brown and cooked through.

5 Serve the chops with any remaining glaze from the grill pan drizzled over and a spoonful of the ragù.

Pork with golden new potatoes and Savoy cabbage

Serves 2
487 calories per serving

225 g (8 oz) baby new
   potatoes
2 teaspoons clear honey
2 teaspoons wholegrain
   mustard
calorie controlled cooking
   spray
250 g (9 oz) Savoy cabbage,
   shredded
1 teaspoon caraway seeds
2 x 150 g (5½ oz) lean pork
   loin steaks
salt and freshly ground black
   pepper

*Pork and cabbage are traditional partners, served here
with new potatoes.*

1 Bring a saucepan of water to the boil, add the potatoes and
cook for 10–15 minutes or until tender. Drain and set aside.

2 Meanwhile, in a bowl, mix together the honey and
wholegrain mustard.

3 Heat a large, non-stick frying pan and spray with the
cooking spray. Arrange the potatoes in the pan and brown for
about 5 minutes, turning occasionally. Add the cabbage and
caraway seeds, spray again with the cooking spray and fry
for a further 2–3 minutes.

4 Meanwhile, spray a second non-stick frying pan with the
cooking spray, add the pork and cook for 2 minutes on each
side until cooked through. Season, spoon the honey and
mustard over the steaks and add 2 tablespoons of water.
Cook for another minute, turning the pork to coat it in the
glaze. Serve on warm plates with the potatoes and cabbage.

Fish and seafood

Cod and chorizo kebabs

Serves 4

179 calories per serving

85 g packet thinly sliced chorizo or spicy salami, each slice halved

500 g (1 lb 2 oz) cod fillets, skinned and cut in 5 cm (2 inch) cubes

2 tablespoons soy sauce

4 courgettes, each cut into 6 thick diagonal slices

These delicious Spanish-style kebabs mix meat and fish on one skewer. Try serving them with cherry tomatoes.

1 Preheat the grill to hot or heat a griddle pan. Fold one half slice of chorizo and thread it on to a skewer (see Tip, page 36), then add a cube of cod. Repeat until you have 3 or so cubes of cod and 4 halves of sausage per skewer. Make 8 skewers.

2 Pour the soy sauce on a plate and turn the skewers on the plate until they are covered in the sauce. Make sure you brush sauce on to the fish with a pastry brush.

3 Place the skewers on a piece of foil on the grill pan or put them straight on to the hot griddle. (You can also cook them on the barbecue.) Grill for 3–4 minutes, then turn them and brush again with the soy sauce. Grill for a further 3–4 minutes until the fish is cooked through and the chorizo is golden. Grill the courgette slices alongside the kebabs – or thread the slices on to the skewers instead, alternating them with the fish and chorizo.

Cod with salsa

Serves 2
110 calories per serving

**calorie controlled cooking
     spray**
2 x 90 g (3¼ oz) cod steaks
½ teaspoon cumin seeds
**salt and freshly ground black
     pepper**

For the salsa
3 tomatoes, cubed finely
**½ a small red onion, cubed
     finely**
**2 tablespoons fresh coriander,
     chopped**
¼ teaspoon ground cumin
juice of ½ a lime

This makes a very simple but tasty light lunch.

1 Preheat the oven to Gas Mark 4/180°C/fan oven 160°C.
Spray a shallow ovenproof dish with the cooking spray. Place
the cod steaks in the dish and season them. Sprinkle with
cumin seeds and then spray the steaks with cooking spray.
Roast for 15–20 minutes.

2 Meanwhile mix the salsa ingredients together, season, then
cover and set aside.

3 Serve the cooked fish with the salsa.

Herb crusted salmon

Serves 4
304 calories per serving

40 g (1½ oz) ciabatta bread
2 teaspoons dried oregano
1 tablespoon fresh rosemary
 needles
finely grated zest and juice of
 a lemon, plus lemon wedges,
 to serve
1 tablespoon freshly grated
 Parmesan cheese
calorie controlled cooking
 spray
4 x 150 g (5½ oz) salmon
 fillets, skinned

*This is a sophisticated yet easy supper dish. It's delicious
with steamed green beans and broccoli.*

1 Preheat the oven to Gas Mark 6/200°C/fan oven 180°C.
Break the bread into pieces and place in a food processor or
blender. Whizz to fine breadcrumbs, then add the oregano,
rosemary, lemon zest and Parmesan. Blend briefly to combine.

2 Line a baking tray with foil and spray with the cooking spray.
Place the salmon fillets on the tray and divide the topping
between them, covering each one. Drizzle with the lemon juice
and spray with the cooking spray. Bake for 15–20 minutes until
golden and the fish is cooked.

Tip… Make extra topping and freeze it for next time.

Pink trout with pickled cucumber

Serves 1
202 calories per serving

140 g (5 oz) pink sea trout fillet

For the pickled cucumber
60 g (2 oz) cucumber, sliced very thinly into rounds
salt
2 teaspoons white wine vinegar
1 teaspoon caster sugar
1 tablespoon chopped fresh dill
salt and freshly ground black pepper

Serve this deliciously light and summery dish with new potatoes and green beans.

1 To make the pickled cucumber, sprinkle the cucumber with salt then set aside for 15 minutes. Rinse to remove the salt, then drain well. Mix together the white wine vinegar, sugar and 2 teaspoons water in a bowl until the sugar dissolves. Add the cucumber and dill, then turn until mixed together. Season with black pepper and set aside.

2 Half fill a lidded frying pan with water and bring to the boil. Place the trout in the pan and return to the boil. Turn off the heat, cover with the lid, and leave the fish to cook in the hot water for 6–8 minutes.

3 Using a fish slice or spatula, remove the trout from the pan and hold it over some kitchen towel to remove excess water. Season to taste before serving with the pickled cucumber.

Leek and potato rösti with smoked salmon

Serves 4
94 calories per serving

200 g (7 oz) potatoes, grated
1 small leek, shredded finely
calorie controlled cooking spray
110 g (4 oz) smoked salmon
4 tablespoons 0% fat Greek yogurt
2 teaspoons chopped fresh dill
salt and freshly ground black pepper

Crisp fried potato and leeks topped with a slice of smoked salmon make a delicious light snack or starter.

1 Squeeze as much liquid as you can from the potatoes, then pat them dry with kitchen paper. Mix with the leek and season.

2 Lightly coat a non-stick frying pan with the cooking spray and heat until hot. Place 4 spoonfuls of the rösti mixture in the pan and flatten them with the back of a spatula.

3 Cook for 5–8 minutes, turning occasionally, until golden and crispy on both sides. Repeat to make 8 rösti in total.

4 Top the rösti with slices of smoked salmon. Mix together the yogurt and dill, season with black pepper (the salmon will make it salty enough) and drizzle over the top and serve.

Tips... Make 16 smaller rösti, dividing the topping equally, to serve as appetisers with drinks.

Dill and salmon go very well together, but you could use 1 teaspoon of lemon zest, instead of the dill, if you prefer.

Smoked salmon parcels

Serves 4
200 calories per serving

2 teaspoons lemon juice
4 x 150 g (5½ oz) pollock fillets
100 g (3½ oz) smoked salmon, cut into long strips, measuring 2 cm (¾ inch) wide
calorie controlled cooking spray
salt and freshly ground black pepper

For the tartare sauce
2 tablespoons extra light mayonnaise
3 tablespoons virtually fat free fromage frais
1 tablespoon lemon juice
4 cocktail gherkins, chopped roughly
1 teaspoon capers in brine, drained and rinsed
1 tablespoon chopped fresh flat leaf parsley
4 lemon wedges, to serve

These elegant fish parcels come with a light home-made tartare sauce. Serve with peas and roast potatoes.

1 Preheat the oven to Gas Mark 4/180°C/fan oven 160°C. Drizzle a little lemon juice over each pollock fillet and season. Fold both ends of the fillet to meet in the middle. Then wrap a strip of smoked salmon horizontally around each fillet and a second strip vertically, so the fish looks like a parcel wrapped in ribbon.

2 Spray a roasting tray with the cooking spray. Place the fish parcels on the tray, spray with the cooking spray and roast for 12–15 minutes until cooked.

3 Meanwhile, make the tartare sauce by combining all the ingredients with 1 tablespoon of water in a small bowl. Serve each fish parcel with 2 tablespoons of tartare sauce and a wedge of lemon for squeezing over.

Salmon fish cakes

Serves 4 (makes 8 fish cakes)
267 calories per serving
❄

500 g (1 lb 2 oz) potatoes,
cubed
400 g can wild red salmon,
drained, boned, skinned and
flaked
7 g (¼ oz) low fat spread
1 egg, lightly beaten
1½ tablespoons plain flour
calorie controlled cooking
spray
salt and freshly ground black
pepper

For the horseradish relish
4 tablespoons extra light
mayonnaise
1 tablespoon lemon juice
1 tablespoon skimmed milk
1 heaped teaspoon
horseradish sauce

*Comforting warm fish cakes served with a tangy
horseradish relish.*

1 Bring a saucepan of water to the boil, add the potatoes and
cook for 10–15 minutes or until just tender. Drain, then refresh
under cold running water until cool enough to handle. Leave
the potatoes to dry.

2 Meanwhile, in a bowl mix together all the ingredients for the
horseradish relish.

3 Grate the potatoes into a mixing bowl, then stir in the
salmon, low fat spread and egg. Season well. Form the mixture
into 8 fish cakes, dusting each one with the flour.

4 Spray a large, non-stick frying pan with the cooking spray
and cook the fish cakes in batches for 3 minutes on each side
until golden. Keep each batch warm while you cook the rest.
Serve with a spoonful of the horseradish relish on the side.

Tip… Serve with 70 g (2½ oz) cooked peas and carrots per
person.

Zesty tuna pasta

Serves 2
388 calories per serving

zest and juice of a lemon
150 g (5½ oz) dried spaghetti
200 g can tuna steak in brine,
drained
4 tomatoes, de-seeded and
cubed
50 g (1¾ oz) flame-roasted red
peppers from a jar, drained
and cubed
1 tablespoon fresh oregano
leaves
freshly ground black pepper

Adding lemon juice to the pasta water while cooking gives the spaghetti a lovely citrus flavour.

1 Put the lemon juice in a large pan and top up with enough cold water to fill the pan. Bring to the boil, add the spaghetti and cook according to the packet instructions until al dente. Using a ladle, remove about 50 ml (2 fl oz) cooking liquid and reserve. Drain the spaghetti in a colander.

2 Meanwhile, put the tuna, lemon zest, tomatoes and peppers in the spaghetti pan with the reserved cooking liquid. Bring back to a simmer, then stir in the spaghetti until combined and heated through.

3 Season generously with freshly ground black pepper and stir through the oregano. Serve immediately.

Nasi goreng

Serves 1

336 calories per serving

50 g (1¾ oz) dried long grain rice

calorie controlled cooking spray

2 shallots, cubed

50 g (1¾ oz) button mushrooms, sliced

1 red chilli, de-seeded and chopped

1 small carrot, quartered and sliced

75 g (2¾ oz) white cabbage, shredded

1 cm (½ inch) fresh root ginger, chopped finely

100 g (3½ oz) cooked prawns

1 tablespoon tomato ketchup

1 tablespoon light soy sauce

freshly ground black pepper

a few watercress sprigs, to garnish

This popular Indonesian dish is also ideal for using up any leftover cooked rice (see Tip). If you are using leftover rice, reheat it until piping hot.

1 Bring a pan of water to the boil, add the rice and cook according to the packet instructions until tender.

2 Meanwhile, heat a wok or non-stick frying pan until hot. Spray with the cooking spray and stir-fry the shallots over a medium heat for 2 minutes.

3 Add the mushrooms, chilli, carrot, cabbage and ginger, spray again with the cooking spray, and stir-fry for 3–4 minutes, adding a splash of water if they start to stick.

4 Stir in the rice, prawns, ketchup and soy sauce and stir until combined and heated through. Season with black pepper and serve garnished with watercress.

Tip… It's useful to know that 50 g (1¾ oz) dried rice is equivalent to 140 g (5 oz) cooked rice.

Ⓥ Variation… Replace the prawns with 75 g (2¾ oz) marinated tofu pieces. Add the tofu in step 3 with the vegetables.

Seared tuna with Chinese noodles

Serves 4

475 calories per serving

250 g (9 oz) thread egg
noodles

4 x 150 g (5½ oz) fresh tuna
steaks

2 teaspoons sunflower oil

2 tablespoons medium sherry

1 small red onion, sliced

1 carrot, cut into thin sticks

100 g (3½ oz) shiitake
mushrooms, sliced

100 g (3½ oz) canned bamboo
shoots, drained and sliced

1 garlic clove, crushed

2.5 cm (1 inch) fresh root
ginger, peeled and grated

2 tablespoons dark soy sauce

Try this simple way to cook fresh tuna, served with stir-fried noodles and vegetables.

1 Place the noodles in a bowl. Pour boiling water over to cover them and allow to soak for 10 minutes. Drain well.

2 Rinse the tuna steaks and pat dry with kitchen towel. Brush a heavy-based pan or griddle pan with a little of the oil and heat until just smoking.

3 Add the tuna steaks and cook for 2–3 minutes per side. When just cooked, add 1 tablespoon of the sherry and allow the pan juices to bubble. Remove from the heat.

4 Heat the remaining oil in a wok and stir-fry the red onion, carrot and mushrooms for 2–3 minutes.

5 Add the drained noodles, bamboo shoots, garlic, ginger, soy sauce and remaining sherry. Stir-fry for 2–3 minutes, pile on to warm plates and top with a tuna steak.

Tip… Tuna is at its best served slightly underdone in the centre. If you don't like it like this, cook for an extra minute per side.

Moules marinières

Serves 1
230 calories per serving

350 g (12 oz) live mussels
1 teaspoon olive oil
2 spring onions, chopped
   finely
1 garlic clove, chopped finely
50 ml (2 fl oz) dry white wine
½ fish or vegetable stock
   cube, dissolved in 50 ml
   (2 fl oz) boiling water
1 small tomato, skinned and
   chopped
freshly ground black pepper
1 tablespoon chopped fresh
   flat leaf parsley, to garnish

*A classic French recipe. Serve with crusty French bread to
mop up the juices.*

1 Scrub the mussels with a small stiff brush and scrape away
their beards with a sharp knife. Throw away any damaged
mussels or ones that remain open when tapped.

2 Heat the oil in a large saucepan. Sauté the spring onions and
garlic for about 3 minutes, until softened. Add the wine, stock
and tomato, and heat until bubbling. Now tip in the mussels.

3 Cover and cook for 3–4 minutes, until the shells have
opened. Discard any mussels that remain shut.

4 Serve the mussels with the wine and garlic pan juices,
seasoned with black pepper and garnished with the chopped
fresh parsley.

Spaghetti vongole

Serves 2

439 calories per serving

575 g (1 lb 4 oz) fresh clams
125 g (4½ oz) dried spaghetti
2 teaspoons olive oil
3 garlic cloves, chopped finely
3 tomatoes, de-seeded and cubed
½ red chilli, de-seeded and chopped finely
2 tablespoons chopped fresh flat leaf parsley
150 ml (5 fl oz) dry white wine
freshly ground black pepper

This dish is a real treat made with fresh clams, but if they are out of season, use 200 g (7 oz) canned clams instead.

1 If you are using clams in shells, discard any clams with broken shells and those that remain open when tapped. Rinse the clams in plenty of cold running water.

2 Bring a saucepan of water to the boil, add the pasta and cook, following the packet instructions, until al dente. Drain.

3 Meanwhile, heat the olive oil in a large, lidded, deep sided sauté or non-stick frying pan. Cook the garlic, tomatoes, chilli and half the parsley for 1–2 minutes, then pour in the wine and boil gently for 2 minutes.

4 Add the clams to the pan, cover, and cook for 4–5 minutes, shaking the pan occasionally until the clams open. Discard any that haven't opened. Remove the clam meat from most of the shells, reserving a few shell-on clams to garnish with.

5 Toss the pasta into the pan and season with black pepper. Serve immediately, sprinkled with the remaining parsley and the shell-on clams.

Vegetarian

Bubble and squeak patties

Serves 2 (makes 6 patties)
248 calories per serving
Ⓥ

500 g (1 lb 2 oz) potatoes,
  peeled and cubed
4 spring onions, sliced
calorie controlled cooking
  spray
100 g (3½ oz) cabbage,
  shredded
1 medium egg, beaten
salt and freshly ground black
  pepper

*You can also use leftover cooked potatoes or mash for
these crisp patties, which cuts down on preparation time.*

1 Bring a pan of water to the boil, add the potatoes and cook
for 10–12 minutes until tender. Drain and mash.

2 Meanwhile, in a medium lidded pan, fry the spring onions in
the cooking spray until they start to soften. Stir in the cabbage,
seasoning and 3 tablespoons of water. Cover the pan and cook
for 4–5 minutes until tender.

3 Mix the vegetables into the mash, adding the beaten egg
and seasoning to taste. Shape the mixture into 6 patties. Heat
a large non-stick frying pan and spray with the cooking spray.
Fry the patties for about 3 minutes each side until golden and
crisp. Serve immediately.

Broad bean tabbouleh with halloumi

Serves 4

334 calories per serving

Ⓥ

150 g (5½ oz) frozen broad beans

125 g (4½ oz) bulgur wheat

6 tomatoes, de-seeded and cut into bite size pieces

5 spring onions, sliced

1 small cucumber, de-seeded and cubed

35 g packet fresh mint, chopped

35 g packet fresh flat leaf parsley, chopped

juice of a lemon

½ teaspoon dried chilli flakes (optional)

250 g (9 oz) light halloumi cheese, sliced into 8

calorie controlled cooking spray

salt and freshly ground black pepper

Serve this herby salad at room temperature with the slices of freshly grilled halloumi on top.

1 Bring a saucepan of water to the boil, add the broad beans and cook for 1–2 minutes until tender. Leave to cool, then remove the tough outer skins, if you like, to reveal the bright green bean.

2 Meanwhile, put the bulgur wheat in a lidded saucepan and cover with plenty of boiling water from the kettle. Bring back to the boil then reduce the heat, cover and simmer for about 10 minutes or until tender. Drain, if necessary, and transfer to a serving bowl.

3 Add the cooked broad beans, tomatoes, spring onions, cucumber, mint and parsley to the serving bowl. Squeeze over the lemon juice, add the chilli flakes (if using) and season well. Stir until combined.

4 Heat a non-stick griddle pan or frying pan. Spray the halloumi with the cooking spray and cook for 4 minutes on each side or until golden. Serve on top of the tabbouleh.

Cherry tomato pizza

Serves 1
431 calories per serving

This is a cheat's version of a classic Italian pizza in superfast time.

60 g (2 oz) self-raising flour
a pinch of salt
15 g (½ oz) low fat spread
a pinch of dried Mediterranean herbs, e.g. oregano, marjoram or basil
4 tablespoons skimmed milk
calorie controlled cooking spray
about 10 cherry tomatoes, halved
40 g (1½ oz) half fat Cheddar cheese, grated
salt and freshly ground black pepper
fresh basil leaves, to garnish

1 Preheat the oven to Gas Mark 7/220°C/fan oven 200°C. Place a baking sheet in the oven to heat up. Sieve the flour into a bowl and mix in the salt. Add the low fat spread in pieces and rub together with your fingertips until it is evenly distributed. Stir in the herbs.

2 Make a well in the centre, pour in the milk and gradually stir it into the mixture. Pull together with your fingers to form a rough dough ball. Add a little more milk if necessary but take care not to make the dough too wet; it just needs to stick together.

3 Spray the heated baking sheet with the cooking spray and place the dough on the baking sheet. Push with your fingers and roll with a rolling pin to form a circle about 5 mm (¼ inch) thick. Pile on the tomatoes, sprinkle with the cheese and season. Bake for 10–12 minutes, until golden around the edges. Serve hot, scattered with fresh basil leaves.

Tip… You can buy thin crust 23 cm (9 inch) pizza bases from the supermarket instead of making your own. Simply pile on the topping above and cook according to the packet instructions.

Butternut squash, spinach and feta lasagne

Serves 2
378 calories per serving

Ⓥ

450 g (1 lb) butternut squash, peeled, de-seeded and cut into 1 cm (½ inch) cubes

calorie controlled cooking spray

150 g (5½ oz) cherry or baby plum tomatoes, halved

225 g (8 oz) spinach leaves, washed

3 fresh egg lasagne sheets, measuring 20 x 15 cm (8 x 6 inches), cut in half

2 tablespoons red or green reduced fat pesto

75 g (2¾ oz) light feta cheese

salt and freshly ground black pepper

fresh basil leaves, to garnish

The simple way to get an utterly delicious lasagne on the table in 30 minutes.

1 Preheat the oven to Gas Mark 6/200°C/fan oven 180°C. Put the butternut squash in a roasting tin and spray with the cooking spray, tossing to coat lightly. Roast for 20 minutes, or until the squash is just tender, then add the tomatoes and roast for 5 more minutes.

2 Meanwhile, cook the spinach in a small amount of water for 2–3 minutes, until the leaves have wilted. Drain well, squeezing out the excess moisture with the back of a spoon. At the same time, bring a large pan of water to the boil, add the lasagne and cook for 3–4 minutes.

3 Remove the squash and tomatoes from the oven. Stir the pesto through them and season.

4 Drain the lasagne sheets well, and layer them on to two warm plates with the squash mixture and the spinach. Sprinkle the feta on top, drizzle over any remaining roasting juices, then serve garnished with the basil leaves.

Tip... To use dried lasagne sheets, cook them for a few minutes longer and then cut them in half once they are cooked.

Chunky Thai vegetable curry

Serves 4
117 calories per serving
Ⓥ

For the paste
1 teaspoon ground coriander
1 small red onion, chopped
a stalk of lemongrass, chopped
2 garlic cloves, crushed
1 bird's eye chilli, de-seeded and chopped roughly
2 cm (¾ inch) fresh root ginger, peeled and chopped

For the curry
calorie controlled cooking spray
250 g (9 oz) sweet potato, cubed
150 g (5½ oz) broccoli florets
150 g (5½ oz) cauliflower florets
1 red pepper, de-seeded and sliced
150 g (5½ oz) baby corn
250 ml (9 fl oz) vegetable stock

This uses an oil-free curry paste that can be made in advance and kept in the fridge for up to 5 days.

1 To make the paste, place all the ingredients in a food processor and blend until they form a coarse paste.

2 Lightly coat a large non-stick frying pan with the cooking spray and heat until hot. Add the paste and stir-fry for 1 minute. Add all the vegetables and cook, stirring, for 2–3 minutes.

3 Add the stock, reduce the heat and simmer for 10 minutes until the vegetables are just tender. You may need to add extra water if the mixture gets too dry.

Hot and sour noodles

Serves 2
455 calories per serving
Ⓥ

125 g (4½ oz) rice noodles
calorie controlled cooking
   spray
1 garlic clove, crushed
2.5 cm (1 inch) fresh root
   ginger, peeled and sliced
   into matchsticks
125 g (4½ oz) canned bamboo
   shoots, rinsed and sliced
   into matchsticks
2 carrots, sliced into
   matchsticks
125 g (4½ oz) beansprouts
1 small red cabbage, shredded
2 tablespoons soy sauce
2 tablespoons plum sauce
2 teaspoons sesame oil
juice of ½ a lime
100 g (3½ oz) radishes, sliced
   finely
a small bunch of fresh
   coriander, chopped

A big plate of crunchy stir-fried vegetables and noodles for supper for two.

1 Cook the noodles as instructed on the packet, or place them in a bowl and cover with boiling water. Leave them to stand for 10 minutes, gently breaking them up after 5 minutes, then drain.

2 Meanwhile, heat a large non-stick frying pan or wok, spray with the cooking spray and stir-fry the garlic and ginger for a few seconds, until they are golden. Add the bamboo shoots and stir-fry for a further 5 minutes on a high heat, then add the other vegetables and stir-fry for 5 minutes more, until they begin to char on the edges.

3 Add the noodles, soy sauce, plum sauce, sesame oil and lime juice. Stir together. Stir in the radishes and coriander and serve.

Leek and potato tortilla

Serves 4

220 calories per serving

225 g (8 oz) potatoes, sliced
350 g (12 oz) leeks, sliced
5 eggs
4 tablespoons skimmed milk
1 teaspoon chopped fresh dill
1 tablespoon sunflower oil
salt and freshly ground black pepper

A leftover slice of this filling tortilla also makes a great packed lunch.

1 Cook the potato slices and leeks in a pan of lightly salted water for 5 minutes, until just tender. Drain well.

2 Beat together the eggs, milk, dill and seasoning.

3 Preheat the grill to a medium heat. Heat the oil in a 20 cm (8 inch) non-stick frying pan and arrange the drained leeks and potato slices over the base. Pour in the egg mixture and cook over a medium heat until you see the edges of the egg setting. Place the pan under the grill to set and finish cooking the top of the omelette.

4 Allow to stand for 5 minutes before carefully turning out on to a serving plate and cutting into wedges.

Tip... If possible use a frying pan with a metal handle. If you don't have one, protect the handle with a double thickness of foil wrapped around it when you put it under the grill.

Variation... Add other cooked vegetables such as cubed peppers, sliced courgettes or mushrooms.

Creamy potato, cauliflower and chick pea korma

Serves 4
305 calories per serving

Ⓥ

❄ (before adding the yogurt)

450 g (1 lb) new potatoes, quartered

1 cauliflower, broken into florets

1 large onion, sliced

395 g jar 98% fat free korma sauce

400 g can chick peas, drained

100 g (3½ oz) baby spinach

4 tablespoons low fat natural yogurt

2 tablespoons chopped fresh coriander

salt

A mild and creamy vegetable curry, yet still perfectly warming for a chilly winter's evening. Serve with naan bread and pickles.

1 Cook the potatoes in boiling water for 5 minutes. Add the cauliflower and onion. Cook for a further 10 minutes or until the vegetables are tender. Drain and return to the pan.

2 Stir in the korma sauce. Heat through gently. Stir in the chick peas and spinach. Cover and simmer for 10 minutes.

3 Season with salt, stir in the yogurt and coriander, and serve.

Macaroni cheese

Serves 2
411 calories per serving
Ⓥ

125 g (4½ oz) dried macaroni
25 g (1 oz) low fat spread
25 g (1 oz) plain flour
150 ml (5 fl oz) vegetable stock
150 ml (5 fl oz) skimmed milk
salt and freshly ground black pepper
½ teaspoon Dijon mustard
40 g (1½ oz) half fat mature Cheddar cheese, grated
1 teaspoon thyme leaves
6 cherry tomatoes, halved
2 teaspoons grated fresh Parmesan cheese

Classic comfort food, this macaroni cheese is pepped up with the addition of tangy tomatoes and fresh thyme.

1 Preheat the oven to Gas Mark 6/200°C/fan oven 180°C. Cook the macaroni in a large pan of boiling water for 10 minutes or until just tender.

2 Meanwhile, place the low fat spread, flour, stock and milk in a small saucepan and warm over a medium heat. Season, then using a whisk or a wooden spoon, stir constantly until the sauce becomes smooth and thickens as it comes to the boil. Reduce the heat and simmer for 3 minutes to cook out the raw flavour of the flour.

3 Remove from the heat and stir in the Dijon mustard and the Cheddar cheese until melted. Drain the pasta and mix into the cheese sauce, then transfer to an ovenproof dish.

4 Scatter the thyme, cherry tomatoes and Parmesan over the top and bake for 15 minutes until golden brown and crisp.

Mexican beans in tortilla baskets

Serves 4

238 calories per serving

Ⓥ

❄ (bean mixture only)

calorie controlled cooking spray

1 onion, chopped finely

2 large garlic cloves, chopped finely

1 large red pepper, de-seeded and cubed

1 courgette, sliced

2 teaspoons fajita seasoning mix

2 teaspoons ground cumin

400 g can kidney beans, drained and rinsed

600 g (1 lb 5 oz) canned chopped tomatoes

2 tablespoons tomato ketchup

4 large soft flour tortillas

4 tablespoons quark

160 g (5¾ oz) avocado flesh

salt and freshly ground black pepper

An eye-catching way to serve spicy Mexican beans.

1 Preheat the oven to Gas Mark 4/180°C/fan oven 160°C. Heat a lidded saucepan and lightly spray with the cooking spray. Add the onion and cook, covered, for 5 minutes, adding a little water if it starts to stick.

2 Stir in the garlic, pepper and courgette, then cook for another 5 minutes. Stir in the spice mix, cumin and kidney beans, followed by the tomatoes and ketchup. Partially cover the pan with the lid and simmer for 10 minutes, stirring occasionally. Season.

3 Meanwhile, microwave the tortillas for 15–20 seconds each. Stand four heatproof mugs upside down on a baking sheet. Spray the outside of the mugs liberally with the cooking spray. Carefully drape the tortillas over the top, shaping the sides to make a basket. Bake for 6 minutes until golden and crisp.

4 Meanwhile, mash the quark and avocado together.

5 Leave the tortillas to cool slightly then remove them from the mugs, hold upright and spoon in the bean mixture. Serve immediately topped, with mashed avocado.

Moorish tagine

Serves 4
259 calories per serving
Ⓥ
❄

calorie controlled cooking
  spray
1 onion, chopped
500 ml (18 fl oz) hot vegetable
  stock
300 g (10½ oz) sweet potato,
  cubed into small pieces
100 g (3½ oz) fine green
  beans, halved
1 red pepper, de-seeded and
  sliced
2 teaspoons ras el hanout or
  any Moroccan spice blend
100 g (3½ oz) dried couscous
410 g can chick peas, drained
  and rinsed
50 g (1¾ oz) raisins

Ras el hanout means 'head of the shop' and every
Moroccan spice seller has their own secret blend of this
traditional spice.

1 Heat a wide, lidded, non-stick saucepan and spray with the cooking spray. Cook the onion for 3–4 minutes until beginning to soften. Add the vegetable stock and sweet potato and bring to the boil. Cover and simmer for 10 minutes.

2 Stir in the beans, pepper and Moroccan spice blend. Cover and cook gently for 5 minutes. Stir in the couscous, chick peas and raisins. Cover and take off the heat.

3 Let the tagine stand for 5 minutes, then fluff up the couscous with a fork. Serve immediately.

Moroccan eggs

Serves 2
339 calories per serving
Ⓥ

calorie controlled cooking
  spray
1 onion, halved and sliced
  thinly
2 garlic cloves, sliced
1½ teaspoons rose harissa
  paste
½ teaspoon ground coriander
300 ml (10 fl oz) vegetable
  stock
400 g can cherry tomatoes in
  rich tomato juice
2 courgettes, cubed finely
220 g can chick peas in water,
  drained
2 tablespoons chopped fresh
  coriander
2 eggs

Try this spicy veg and egg dish for lunch or a light supper.

1 Heat a lidded non-stick frying pan, spray with the cooking spray and add the onion and garlic. Fry them, stirring constantly, until starting to soften. Add the harissa paste and ground coriander, stir well then pour in the vegetable stock. Cover and simmer for 5 minutes.

2 Add the tomatoes and courgettes and cook gently for 10 minutes until the courgettes are tender. Stir in the chick peas and coriander, then make two hollows in the mixture and break in the eggs. Cover and cook for 2 minutes, then allow to settle for a further 2 minutes before serving.

Tip… If you can't find a 220 g can of chick peas, measure out 130 g (4½ oz) drained chick peas from a larger can.

Serve with a medium slice of unbuttered wholewheat toast per person.

Mushrooms with white bean mash

Serves 2

236 calories per serving

Ⓨ

½ red pepper, de-seeded and cut into long slices

2 large portobello mushrooms, stalks removed

calorie controlled cooking spray

1 teaspoon cumin seeds

1 teaspoon olive oil

2 large garlic cloves, chopped

2.5 cm (1 inch) fresh root ginger, peeled and grated

125 g (4½ oz) canned butter beans, drained and rinsed

50 ml (2 fl oz) skimmed milk

2 tablespoons lemon juice

80 g (3 oz) light halloumi cheese, cut into 2 long slices

salt and freshly ground black pepper

Portobello mushrooms filled with cumin-spiced butter bean mash and topped with grilled halloumi cheese.

1 Preheat the grill to high and line the grill pan with foil. Place the peppers and mushrooms, gill-side up, on the foil. Spray with the cooking spray and grill for 4–5 minutes. Turn everything over, spray again, and grill for another 4–5 minutes until tender and the pepper is charred in places.

2 Meanwhile, toast the cumin seeds in a dry non-stick saucepan for 2 minutes, then add the olive oil, garlic and ginger to the pan and cook for a minute. Add the butter beans and cook for about 5 minutes, stirring, adding a splash of water if they start to stick.

3 Pour in the milk and warm through, then mash the beans to a coarse purée. Stir in the lemon juice and season.

4 Heat a griddle or non-stick frying pan until hot and spray the halloumi with the cooking spray. Cook the halloumi for about 2–3 minutes on each side until golden.

5 Reheat the bean mash and spoon it on top of the mushrooms. Top with a slice of halloumi and red pepper. Season and serve.

Variation… Replace the halloumi with a rasher of lean back bacon per person, grilled until crisp.

Mushroom tortes

Serves 2
227 calories per serving

calorie controlled cooking
  spray
50 g (1¾ oz) Parmesan
  cheese, grated finely
300 g (10½ oz) mixed
  mushrooms such as shiitake,
  chestnut or oyster, trimmed
  and sliced
100 g (3½ oz) low fat soft
  cheese with garlic and herbs
1 egg, beaten
2 tablespoons finely chopped
  fresh flat leaf parsley
salt and freshly ground black
  pepper

*A satisfying and unusual lunch that's ideal for using up
a mixture of mushrooms.*

1 Preheat the oven to Gas Mark 4/180°C/fan oven 160°C and
spray two holes of a 6 hole non-stick jumbo muffin tin, or
two 200 ml (7 oz) ramekins, with the cooking spray. Sprinkle
1 tablespoon of the cheese into the two holes or ramekins
and shake to line the sides. Tip any remaining cheese into
a large bowl and set aside.

2 Heat a non-stick frying pan and spray with the cooking
spray. Add the mushrooms and cook for 5 minutes until starting
to colour and their juices have evaporated. Transfer half the
mixture to a food processor with the soft cheese and whizz
until finely chopped.

3 Transfer the chopped mixture to the bowl with the reserved
cheese and mix together with the egg, parsley, seasoning and
remaining cooked mushrooms. Divide equally between the
two holes of the prepared muffin tin and bake in the oven
for 15 minutes until golden and just set. Transfer to plates
and serve.

Tip... Serve with a wild rocket and tomato salad and 125 g
(4½ oz) boiled potatoes per person.

Piedmont peppers

Serves 2

232 calories per serving

Ⓥ

2 large red peppers, halved
  and de-seeded, stalks intact

16 cherry tomatoes, halved

100 g (3½ oz) light feta
  cheese, cubed

2 tablespoons white balsamic
  vinegar

salt and freshly ground black
  pepper

fresh basil leaves, to garnish

*A flavourful take on stuffed peppers that's so quick to
make.*

1 Preheat the oven to Gas Mark 4/180°C/fan oven 160°C and
place the peppers, skin side down, on a baking tray. In a bowl,
toss the tomatoes with the other ingredients and fill the pepper
shells with this mixture.

2 Bake for 20 minutes, until softened and slightly charred,
then serve scattered with basil.

Ratatouille pasta

Serves 4
332 calories per serving
Ⓥ

calorie controlled cooking
  spray
1 red onion, chopped roughly
1 red pepper, de-seeded and
  chopped roughly
1 yellow pepper, de-seeded
  and chopped roughly
2 courgettes, cubed
1 aubergine, cubed
3 garlic cloves, crushed
400 g can chopped tomatoes
200 g (7 oz) dried fusilli or
  conchiglie
100 g (3½ oz) Brie, sliced
  thinly
freshly ground black pepper

*The melted Brie topping adds a creamy richness to this
tasty dish.*

1 Heat a large, lidded saucepan until hot and spray with
the cooking spray. Cook the onion for 2 minutes, then add
the peppers and cook for 2 minutes more, stirring. Add the
courgettes, aubergine and garlic and cook for 3 minutes.
Add a splash of water if necessary, to prevent the vegetables
from sticking to the pan.

2 Cover the pan and cook for a further 4 minutes over
a medium heat, until the vegetables have softened, then add
the tomatoes and simmer for 10 minutes, uncovered. Season
with black pepper.

3 Meanwhile, bring a large pan of water to the boil, add the
pasta and cook according to the packet instructions, until
tender. Preheat the grill.

4 Drain the pasta and mix with the ratatouille. Tip into an
ovenproof baking dish and top with the sliced Brie. Grill for
2–3 minutes until the Brie starts to melt. Serve on warm plates.

Root vegetable rösti with poached egg

Serves 1

327 calories per serving

Ⓥ

❄ (rosti, cooked or uncooked)

220 g (7½ oz) potatoes, unpeeled and halved

125 g (4½ oz) celeriac, cut into large chunks

100 g (3½ oz) carrots, cut into thirds

calorie controlled cooking spray

1 large egg

salt and freshly ground black pepper

a handful of rocket leaves, to serve

Try this for brunch at the weekend.

1 Bring a pan of water to the boil and cook the potatoes for about 10 minutes until almost tender. Drain, refresh under cold running water, drain again, then leave to cool. Peel the potatoes once cool.

2 Meanwhile, steam the celeriac and carrots for about 4 minutes or until almost tender. Refresh under cold running water, drain, and leave to cool. When the vegetables are cool, grate them coarsely into a bowl, along with the potatoes, and season well. Firmly press the potato mixture into two small flat patties using your hands, leaving the edges fairly ragged.

3 Spray a large, heavy-based frying pan with the cooking spray and fry the rösti for 6–10 minutes on each side until golden and cooked through.

4 Meanwhile, poach the egg until the white is firm and the yolk is still slightly runny. To serve, place one rösti on a plate. Add some rocket leaves, followed by the other rösti and place the poached egg on top.

Sweetcorn fritters with sweet and sour vegetables

Serves 4
203 calories per serving
Ⓥ

For the fritters
326 g can sweetcorn, drained
7 spring onions, chopped finely
2 teaspoons soy sauce
3 tablespoons plain flour
1 large egg, separated
calorie controlled cooking spray
salt and freshly ground black pepper

For the vegetables
1 tablespoon Chinese rice vinegar
1 tablespoon caster sugar
3 tablespoons soy sauce
2 onions, sliced
12 baby corn, halved lengthways
150 g (5½ oz) mange tout
150 g (5½ oz) chestnut mushrooms, sliced
2 garlic cloves, chopped
2 pak choi, sliced lengthways
2 handfuls of beansprouts

These simple fritters go perfectly with the Chinese-style stir-fried veg.

1 In a bowl, mix together the sweetcorn, spring onions, soy sauce, flour and egg yolk. Season. In a clean, grease-free bowl, whisk the egg white until it forms stiff peaks, then gently fold it into the sweetcorn mixture using a metal spoon.

2 Heat a large, non-stick frying pan and coat with the cooking spray. Using 3 tablespoons of batter per fritter, cook four fritters at a time, flattening each slightly with a spatula. Cook for 2–3 minutes on each side until golden. Keep warm while you cook the second batch to make eight fritters in total.

3 For the sweet and sour vegetables, in a bowl mix the rice vinegar, sugar and soy sauce with 3 tablespoons of water and set aside. Heat a wok or large non-stick frying pan and spray with the cooking spray. Stir-fry the onions for 3 minutes then add the baby corn, mange tout, mushrooms, garlic and pak choi, and stir-fry for another 2 minutes.

4 Stir in the rice vinegar mixture and cook for 1 minute before tossing in the beansprouts. Serve with the fritters.

Vegetable frittata

Serves 4

317 calories per serving

Frittatas are great one-pan meals and leftovers are ideal for snacks or lunchboxes.

500 g (1 lb 2 oz) new potatoes, halved if large

calorie controlled cooking spray

3 onions, chopped

1 teaspoon dried Mediterranean herbs

110 g (4 oz) baby spinach leaves

10 cherry tomatoes, halved

1 heaped teaspoon Dijon mustard

6 large eggs, beaten

salt and freshly ground black pepper

1 Cook the potatoes in plenty of boiling water until tender, then drain and leave to cool slightly before peeling. Cut the potatoes into bite size chunks.

2 Meanwhile, spray a 25 cm (10 inch) heavy-based frying pan with the cooking spray and fry the onions for 10 minutes until softened, adding a little water if necessary. Stir in the herbs.

3 While the onions are cooking, steam the spinach and squeeze thoroughly to remove any water, then chop roughly.

4 Preheat the grill to medium hot. Add the spinach and potatoes to the frying pan so they are evenly spread over the base of the pan. Arrange the tomatoes in the pan. Season well.

5 Stir the mustard into the eggs and pour the mixture over the top of the vegetables. Cook on the hob over a low heat for 8–10 minutes, until the base is set and golden, then brown the top under the grill for 5 minutes.

Spicy bean cakes with onion relish

Serves 4

231 calories per serving

Ⓥ

❄ (bean cakes only)

calorie controlled cooking
  spray
2 onions, 1½ sliced finely and
  ½ chopped finely
1 tablespoon grated fresh root
  ginger
2 tablespoons balsamic
  vinegar
200 ml (7 fl oz) boiling water
1 red pepper, de-seeded and
  cubed
2 x 410 g cans black eyed
  beans, rinsed and drained
1 egg, beaten
2 teaspoons curry powder
salt and freshly ground black
  pepper

Piquant bean cakes served with a delicious onion relish.

1 To make the onion relish, spray a lidded, non-stick saucepan
with the cooking spray. Fry the sliced onions for 5 minutes.
Add half the ginger, the balsamic vinegar and the boiling water.
Cover and simmer for 5 minutes, then remove the lid. Cook
rapidly for a further 10 minutes until the onions are tender and
almost all of the liquid has evaporated.

2 Meanwhile, spray a non-stick frying pan with the cooking
spray. Fry the chopped onion with the pepper and the rest of
the ginger for 4 minutes until caramelised.

3 Tip three quarters of the beans and the egg into a food
processor. Whizz to a paste then transfer the mixture to a bowl.
Stir the curry powder into the pepper and onions and cook for
a few seconds, then tip this into the bowl, along with the rest
of the beans and season. Bring the mixture together by hand
and shape into 8 cakes.

4 Rinse the frying pan, return to the heat and spray with
cooking spray. Fry the bean cakes for 3 minutes on each side
until golden brown and crusty. Serve with the onion relish.

Zesty tofu noodles

Serves 4
296 calories per serving
Ⓥ

grated zest and juice of a lime
1 tablespoon soy sauce
2 tablespoons sweet chilli
   sauce
calorie controlled cooking
   spray
4 spring onions, sliced
1 orange or red pepper,
   de-seeded and sliced thinly
225 g can bamboo shoots in
   water, drained
2 garlic cloves, chopped
1 red chilli, de-seeded and
   chopped
160 g (5¾ oz) marinated tofu
   pieces
2 x 150 g packets straight-to-
   wok rice ribbon noodles
200 g (7 oz) beansprouts
1 tablespoon chopped roasted
   peanuts
4 tablespoons chopped fresh
   coriander
1 egg, beaten

This dish uses marinated tofu rather than the plain type,
which many people find too bland.

1 In a bowl, mix the lime zest and juice with the soy sauce,
chilli sauce and 3 tablespoons of water.

2 Heat a non-stick wok, spray with the cooking spray and
add the spring onions, pepper, bamboo shoots, garlic and chilli.
Stir-fry for 5 minutes until the vegetables begin to soften.

3 Pour the lime mixture into the pan, then add the tofu, noodles
and beansprouts and stir well over the heat to mix everything
together. Cook until everything is piping hot, about 3–5 minutes,
and then take the pan off the heat and toss in the peanuts,
coriander and beaten egg. The egg will cook instantly as it gets
tossed into the hot noodles. Serve immediately.

Desserts and bakes

Raspberry tarts

Makes 4
142 calories per tart

These cheeky little tarts have a wonderful surprise waiting for you at the bottom – delicious jammy raspberries.

calorie controlled cooking
  spray
4 x 25 g (1 oz) filo pastry
  sheets (about 24 cm/
  9½ inches square)
3 teaspoons seedless
  raspberry jam
75 g (2¾ oz) fresh raspberries
150 g pot ready-made low fat
  custard
1 egg, beaten

1 Preheat the oven to Gas Mark 4/180°C/fan oven 160°C. In a 6 hole muffin tin, spray 4 holes with the cooking spray. Take one sheet of filo pastry and spray with the cooking spray. Fold it into quarters to make a 12 cm (4½ inches) square. Use this to line 1 hole in the tin. Repeat with the remaining filo sheets to line 4 holes in total.

2 Mix the jam with half of the raspberries and spoon a quarter of the mixture into the base of each tart. In a jug, mix together the custard and beaten egg and pour equal amounts into the tart cases until the mixture is used up.

3 Scatter the remaining raspberries over the top of each tart and bake in the oven for 15–20 minutes until just set. Serve warm or leave to cool.

Variation... You can use other flavours of jam – strawberry or blackcurrant are delicious too.

Apple and raspberry muffins

Makes 12
162 calories per muffin

Enjoy a deliciously moist muffin with a cup of tea.

calorie controlled cooking spray
225 g (8 oz) self-raising flour
1 teaspoon bicarbonate of soda
a pinch of salt
25 g (1 oz) porridge oats
100 g (3½ oz) caster sugar
150 g (5½ oz) apple sauce
3 tablespoons sunflower oil
175 g (6 oz) low fat natural yogurt
6 tablespoons skimmed milk
1 egg, beaten
100 g (3½ oz) raspberries, fresh or frozen (see Tip)

1 Preheat the oven to Gas Mark 6/200°C/fan oven 180°C. Lightly grease a non-stick 12 hole muffin tin with the cooking spray or simply use 12 paper cases in the holes in the tin.

2 Sift the flour, bicarbonate of soda and salt into a mixing bowl. Reserve 1 tablespoon of oats, then stir the remaining oats and sugar into the flour.

3 In a separate bowl, mix the apple sauce, oil, yogurt, milk and egg together, then stir this wet mixture into the dry ingredients, mixing until just combined but still slightly lumpy. Stir in the raspberries, then spoon the mixture into the muffin tins, dividing it evenly. Scatter with the reserved oats and bake in the oven for 20 minutes until risen, firm and golden brown.

4 Cool the muffins on a wire rack before serving.

Tips… Look out for reusable silicone muffin cases. You don't need to grease them, yet they'll still easily peel away from your baked muffins.

Frozen berries can be stirred straight into the batter; there's no need to defrost them first.

Variation… Use 100 g (3½ oz) blueberries instead of raspberries. Add a pinch of ground cinnamon too.

Cappuccino muffins

Makes 6
201 calories per muffin
Ⓥ
❄ (un-iced muffins)

For the muffins
75 g (2¾ oz) low fat spread
50 g (1¾ oz) light soft brown sugar
2 eggs
75 g (2¾ oz) self-raising flour
3 teaspoons cocoa
1 tablespoon instant coffee granules
30 g (1¼ oz) walnut pieces, chopped finely
calorie controlled cooking spray

For the icing
125 g (4½ oz) quark
1 teaspoon vanilla extract
30 g (1¼ oz) icing sugar, sieved

These scrummy muffins are perfect with a coffee and look just like a cappuccino.

1 Preheat the oven to Gas Mark 5/190°C/fan oven 170°C. In a bowl, whisk together the low fat spread and sugar using an electric hand whisk, then whisk in the eggs, flour and 2 teaspoons of the cocoa until combined.

2 Dissolve the coffee in 1 tablespoon of water then fold into the cake mixture along with the walnuts. Spray a 6 hole non-stick muffin tin with the cooking spray and divide the mixture equally between the holes. Bake for 15 minutes until golden and the tops spring back when pressed.

3 Meanwhile, mix together the quark, vanilla extract and icing sugar until smooth and chill it in the fridge.

4 Turn the muffins out on to a wire rack. If serving warm, swirl the quark icing on top of each muffin and dust with the remaining cocoa. If serving cold, leave the muffins to go cold before icing.

Cherry scones

Makes 12
100 calories per scone

Ⓥ
❄

1 tablespoon lemon juice
150 ml (5 fl oz) skimmed milk
225 g (8 oz) self-raising flour
½ teaspoon cream of tartar
salt
40 g (1½ oz) low fat spread
25 g (1 oz) caster sugar
60 g (2 oz) glacé cherries, chopped
calorie controlled cooking spray

These scones have a superbly light texture and are absolutely irresistible.

1 Preheat the oven to Gas Mark 6/200°C/fan oven 180°C. Mix the lemon juice with the milk and set aside to thicken and curdle. Set aside 1 teaspoon of flour for rolling out, then sift the remaining flour, cream of tartar and a pinch of salt into a bowl.

2 Rub in the low fat spread until the mixture looks like crumbs, then stir in the sugar and cherries. Make a well in the centre.

3 Reserve 2 tablespoons of the milk to brush the tops of the scones, then mix enough of the remaining milk into the flour mixture to give a soft but not sticky dough.

4 Dust the work surface with the reserved flour and roll out the dough to 2 cm (¾ inch) deep. Cut out 12 x 5 cm (2 inch) scones using a cutter, re-rolling the scone dough as needed.

5 Place the scones on a baking tray, lightly greased with the cooking spray, then brush the tops with the reserved milk. Bake for 12–15 minutes until well risen and golden brown. Cool slightly on a wire rack before serving.

Nutty bran muffins

Makes 9
58 calories per muffin

Ⓥ
❄

75 g (2¾ oz) bran flakes
200 ml (7 fl oz) hot skimmed milk
150 g (5½ oz) self-raising flour
1 teaspoon bicarbonate of soda
75 g (2¾ oz) ready-to-eat dried exotic fruits, chopped finely
2 eggs, beaten
50 g (1¾ oz) low fat spread, melted
15 g (½ oz) demerara sugar

This is the perfect way to eat breakfast on the go.

1 Preheat the oven to Gas Mark 5/190°C/fan oven 170°C and line a 12 hole muffin tin with 9 paper cases. Put the bran flakes in a bowl and pour over the hot milk. Leave to soak for 5 minutes.

2 Meanwhile, in a bowl, mix together the flour, bicarbonate of soda and chopped fruits. Stir in the eggs, melted low fat spread, soaked bran flakes and leftover milk until combined.

3 Divide the mixture between the paper cases, sprinkle with the sugar and bake for 15–20 minutes until golden and risen. Leave to cool on a wire rack.

Tip… Enjoy with a latte made with 150 ml (5 fl oz) skimmed milk.

Variation… Try using other dried fruits such as ready-to-eat dried apple pieces.

Rosemary soda bread

Serves 4
355 calories per serving
Ⓥ

200 g (7 oz) plain white flour
200 g (7 oz) wholemeal flour
1½ teaspoons bicarbonate of soda
1½ teaspoons baking powder
1 tablespoon olive oil spread
1½ teaspoons dried rosemary, chopped finely
½ teaspoon fine sea salt
freshly ground black pepper
250 ml (9 fl oz) skimmed milk

This delicious, aromatic bread tastes as good as it smells. Serve it warm with soup for a lunchtime treat.

1 Preheat the oven to Gas Mark 7/220°C/fan oven 200°C. Put the flours, bicarbonate of soda, baking powder, olive oil spread, rosemary, salt and pepper in a food processor, and blend for about 20 seconds.

2 Tip the mixture into a bowl and gradually mix in the skimmed milk using a table knife to make a firm, but not too dry, dough. Knead lightly until the dough is smooth.

3 Cover a baking sheet with non-stick baking parchment. Shape the dough into a flat round about 20 cm (8 inches) in diameter. With a sharp knife, score a deep cross on top to mark it into four.

4 Bake for about 20 minutes until the bread has risen and is springy to the touch. You can check it is cooked by knocking the underneath – if it sounds hollow, it is ready.

Baked Alaska

Serves 4
245 calories per serving
Ⓥ

18 cm (7 inch) round sponge
  flan case
300 g can raspberries in
  natural juice (or other soft
  fruit), drained
3 medium egg whites
75 g (2¾ oz) caster sugar
480 ml (17½ fl oz) low fat
  vanilla ice cream

This is an impressive dessert that can be made in minutes.
It's a heavenly combination of very hot and very cold with
soft, chewy and crispy textures.

1 Preheat the oven to Gas Mark 8/230°C/fan oven 210°C and
remove all the shelves except for one in the middle.

2 Place the flan case on an ovenproof plate and spoon over
the fruit.

3 Whisk the egg white until stiff then add the sugar and whisk
again until glossy.

4 Scoop the ice cream quickly on top of the fruit. Pile the
meringue mixture over the whole lot, taking it down to the dish
and making little peaks all over the surface by dabbing it with
the back of a spoon or spatula.

5 Place in the oven immediately and cook for 2–3 minutes,
watching carefully and removing immediately once the tips
of the peaks turn golden brown. Serve straight away.

Crunchy apple crumbles

Serves 4
263 calories per serving
Ⓥ

1 cooking apple, peeled, cored
   and cubed
4 eating apples, peeled, cored
   and cubed
juice of ½ a lemon
25 g (1 oz) caster sugar
25 g (1 oz) low fat spread
50 g (1¾ oz) plain flour
50 g (1¾ oz) grape nuts cereal
   or rolled oats
¼ teaspoon ground ginger

These easy individual crumbles are ideal for when you
want something comforting to finish off a meal.

1 Preheat the oven to Gas Mark 5/190°C/fan oven 170°C.
Put the apples, lemon juice, sugar and 2 tablespoons of cold
water into a small, lidded saucepan and bring to the boil.
Cover and simmer for 5 minutes until the cooking apples
are pulpy and the eating apples are tender.

2 Meanwhile, in a bowl, rub together the low fat spread and
flour with your fingertips until it resembles coarse crumbs.
Stir in the cereal or rolled oats.

3 Stir the ground ginger into the apples and then divide
between four 250 ml (9 fl oz) ramekins or ovenproof dishes.
Sprinkle the crumble mixture equally over the top. Bake in
the oven for 10 minutes until golden.

Tip... You can make these in advance and keep them
chilled in the fridge for up to 3 days before baking.

Banana pancakes with plums

Serves 4
256 calories per serving
Ⓥ
❄ (pancakes only)

140 g (5 oz) self-raising flour
1 teaspoon bicarbonate of
  soda
200 ml (7 fl oz) skimmed milk
1 egg
1 large ripe banana, mashed
8 plums, halved and stoned
2 tablespoons apple juice
calorie controlled cooking
  spray
4 tablespoons 0% fat Greek
  yogurt

Mashed banana makes these quick pancakes nice and moist. Serve for dessert or breakfast.

1 In a bowl, sift together the flour and bicarbonate of soda and make a well in the centre. In a jug, whisk the milk with the egg, then gradually pour it into the well, whisking constantly to avoid any lumps. Set aside for 10 minutes, then stir in the mashed banana.

2 Meanwhile, in a small pan, gently cook the plums and apple juice for about 10 minutes until the plums are softened.

3 Heat a large, non-stick frying pan and spray with the cooking spray. For each pancake, spoon 2 tablespoons of the batter into the pan and cook for about 1–1½ minutes on each side until golden. Cook three pancakes at a time, then remove and keep warm. Make 12 pancakes in total.

4 Serve three pancakes per person. Spoon over the plums and a little cooking juice, and serve the yogurt on the side.

Variation… For a savoury version, omit the banana, plums, apple juice and yogurt and serve the pancakes with 2 rashers of lean back bacon each and grilled tomatoes.

Pineapple sticks with chocolate dip

Serves 4
164 calories per serving
Ⓥ

½ a pineapple, about 600 g
(1 lb 5 oz)
5 tablespoons orange juice
1 teaspoon clear honey

For the chocolate dip
2 heaped tablespoons
hazelnut and chocolate
spread
2 heaped tablespoons virtually
fat free fromage frais
1–2 tablespoons skimmed
milk

This is the perfect method to make a little hazelnut and chocolate spread go a long way.

1 Slice the pineapple into 2 cm (¾ inch) thick slices then cut away the skin. Cut each pineapple round into quarters, remove the core and cut the quarters into 2–3 chunks depending on their size.

2 Mix together 4 tablespoons of the orange juice and the honey in a shallow dish and add the pineapple chunks. Toss well until coated. Thread the pineapple lengthways on to metal skewers – about 4–5 pieces per skewer – to make 8 kebabs.

3 Preheat the grill to high and grill the skewers in two batches for about 8 minutes each, turning occasionally, until starting to caramelise.

4 Meanwhile, in a bowl, mix together the remaining orange juice, hazelnut and chocolate spread, fromage frais and milk to achieve a dipping consistency. Serve the pineapple sticks with the chocolate dip.

Index

Other titles in the Weight Watchers Mini Series

ISBN 978-0-85720-932-0

ISBN 978-0-85720-935-1

ISBN 978-0-85720-934-4

ISBN 978-0-85720-938-2

ISBN 978-0-85720-931-3

ISBN 978-0-85720-937-5

ISBN 978-0-85720-936-8

ISBN 978-0-85720-933-7

ISBN 978-1-47111-084-9

ISBN 978-1-47111-089-4

ISBN 978-1-47111-091-7

ISBN 978-1-47111-087-0

ISBN 978-1-47111-090-0

ISBN 978-1-47111-085-6

ISBN 978-1-47111-088-7

ISBN 978-1-47111-086-3

ISBN 978-1-47113-165-3

ISBN 978-1-47113-166-0

ISBN 978-1-47113-167-7

ISBN 978-1-47113-164-6

For more details please visit www.simonandschuster.co.uk